Six Days of Sistine

ACCOMPANIMENT TO THE FILM

POETRY | SCRIPT | PHOTOS | INSPIRATION AND INFLUENCES | LOCATIONS | BEHIND THE SCENES PHOTOS

FOR MARKOSIA ENTERPRISES LTD

HARRY MARKOS
PUBLISHER & MANAGING PARTNER

GM JORDAN
SPECIAL PROJECTS CO-ORDINATOR

ANNIKA EADE
MEDIA MANAGER

ANDY BRIGGS
CREATIVE CONSULTANT

MEIRON JONES
MARKETING DIRECTOR

IAN SHARMAN
EDITOR IN CHIEF

Six Days Of Sistine: Accompaniment To The Film ™ & © 2018 Perry Pictures & Markosia Enterprises, Ltd. All Rights Reserved. Reproduction of any part of this work by any means without the written permission of the publisher is expressly forbidden. All names, characters and events in this publication are entirely fictional. Any resemblance to actual persons, living or dead is purely coincidental. Published by Markosia Enterprises, PO BOX 3477, Barnet, Hertfordshire, EN5 9HN. FIRST PRINTING, October 2020. Harry Markos, Director.

ISBN 978-1-913802-04-2

www.markosia.com

"Dialogue is poetry
in this uniquely wonderful film,
as if the lovers whispered stars."
Nina Welch, (Arizona Film Festival)

PERRY PICTURES PRESENTS 'SIX DAYS OF SISTINE'

JAMIE CAMPBELL BOWER ELARICA JOHNSON AMANDA ABBINGTON

VISUAL EFFECTS SUPERVISOR ALEX MURRAY MUSIC BY TONY ANDERSON EDITED BY MAX MCPHERSON

CASTING BY DANIEL EDWARDS CDG DIRECTOR OF PHOTOGRAPHY ROBIN VIDGEON B.S.C.

PRODUCED BY PETER MACDONALD RICHARD J. PERRY POEMS WRITTEN BY ANDREA DIETRICH

WRITTEN AND DIRECTED BY RICHARD J. PERRY

- CONTENTS -

- CHAPTER ONE -
CAST AND CREW

- CHAPTER TWO -
DIRECTOR'S STATEMENT

- CHAPTER THREE -
FESTIVALS AND AWARDS

- CHAPTER FOUR -
POETRY

- CHAPTER FIVE -
JEAN BAPTISTE AND SISTINE PHOTOS

- CHAPTER SIX -
LOCATIONS

- CHAPTER SEVEN -
BEHIND THE SCENES PHOTOS

- CHAPTER EIGHT -
SCRIPT

- CHAPTER NINE -
MUSIC

- CHAPTER TEN -
INFLUENCES AND INSPIRATIONS

- CHAPTER ELEVEN -
SPECIAL THANKS

- CAST AND CREW -

JEAN-BAPTISTE	JAMIE CAMPBELL BOWER
SISTINE	ELARICA JOHNSON
ANGELINA	AMANDA ABBINGTON
BUCK	HARRY ATTWELL
MAL	CRAIG TALBOT
ENNI	JAMIE LANGLANDS
JAMES	KANE SURRY
MARKETING EXECUTIVE	JACKIE PULFORD
CAR LEAVER	IAN WILLIAMSON
BABY	LUCAS WINDERS
DRESS SELLER	STEPHANIE BOOTY
THE FAMILY	GINA MCSTAY
	JOHN MCSTAY
	MEGAN MCSTAY
	RUBY MCSTAY

DIRECTOR	RICHARD J. PERRY
PRODUCER	PETER MACDONALD
WRITER (SCREENPLAY)	RICHARD J. PERRY
WRITER (POETRY)	ANDREA DIETRICH
CINEMATOGRAPHER	ROBIN VIDGEON B.S.C
CASTING DIRECTOR	DANIEL EDWARDS CDG
MUSIC	TONY ANDERSON
EDITOR	MAX MCPHERSON
MAKEUP	TASHAN CIAN
SPX MAKEUP	BRODIE MAYHEW
ADDITIONAL PHOTOGRAPHY	SIMON LIVINGSTONE
FIRST ASSISTANT CAMERA	EAMONN O'KEEFFE
SECOND ASSISTANT CAMERA	JOSH BLOOMER
ASSISTANT CAMERA	DYLAN HAYES
B CAM ASSISTANT (DAILIES)	MARIA CAMILLA PIANA BRIZIO
DRONE OPERATOR	BRIAN URANOVSKY
STILLS	MARC HANKINS
VFX	ALEX MURRAY
POST-PRODUCTION SUPERVISOR	DAVID O'BRIEN
RE-RECORDING MIXER	DAVID DRAKE
SOUND EFFECTS EDITOR	MICHAEL WILLIAMS
SOUND EDITOR	HARRY PLATFORD

- DIRECTORS STATEMENT -

"THE IDEA FOR SIX DAYS OF SISTINE FIRST CAME WHEN I WAS AT THE NEW YORK METROPOLITAN MUSEUM OF ART,

I JUST SAT AND STARED AT A PAINTING FOR TWO HOURS.

MESMERISED AND LOST IN FINDING OUT NEW TEXTURES AND NEW MEANINGS IN SOMETHING THAT'S JUST ONE FRAME.

I WONDERED IF A MOVIE COULD BE SIMILAR. LIKE AN OIL PAINTING... SOMETHING TO SIMPLY ENJOY AND BE LOST IN ON A SPIRITUAL AND PEACEFUL LEVEL.

THIS WAS A FILM I'VE ALWAYS WANTED TO MAKE.

A FILM THAT EXAMINES LOVE, CLOSENESS, AND SPIRITUAL TOGETHERNESS. ALL THROUGH FEELING AND TOUCH RATHER THAN DIALOGUE.

USING POETRY TO SHOW EXACTLY WHAT THESE CHARACTERS ARE FEELING AND THINKING. IT'S A MAGICAL, SPIRITUAL FILM THAT SHOWS US THE BEAUTY OF COMING TOGETHER AND LOVING ONE ANOTHER.

I HOPE YOU ENJOY THIS BOOK"

RICHARD PERRY

FESTIVALS AND AWARDS

- FESTIVALS AND AWARDS -

WINNER - CALCUTTA FILM FEST
BEST EXPERIMENTAL FILM OUTSTANDING ACHIEVEMENT AWARD

WINNER - OLYMPUS FILM FESTIVAL
BEST EXPERIMENTAL FILM AND BEST ACTOR JAMIE CAMPBELL BOWER

WINNER - VIRGIN SPRING CINE FEST
BRONZE BEST EXPERIMENTAL FILM, SILVER BEST DIRECTOR

WINNER - MADRID FILM FESTIVAL
BEST ACTOR JAMIE CAMPBELL BOWER

WINNER - NEW VISION FILM FESTIVAL
BEST EXPERIMENTAL FILM

OFFICIAL SELECTION
MADRID FILM FESTIVAL
NOMINATED FOR BEST DIRECTOR, BEST FILM, BEST ACTRESS

OFFICIAL SELECTION
ARIZONA FILM FESTIVAL

OFFICIAL SELECTION
NEW VISION FILM FESTIVAL

OFFICIAL SELECTION
NEW HOPE FILM FESTIVAL

OFFICIAL SELECTION
PORTUGAL FILM FESTIVAL

OFFICIAL SELECTION
BRAZIL FILM FESTIVAL

OFFICIAL SELECTION
PRISMA FILM AWARDS

OFFICIAL SELECTION
DUMBO FILM FESTIVAL

OFFICIAL SELECTION
SANTIAGO INDEPENDENT FILM AWARDS

LIST OF POEMS BY ANDREA DIETRICH

A HOME SWEET HOME

A TALE OF FIRE AND ICE

A TRIBUTE TO A STAR

AT THE END OF THE RAINBOW

CINDER GIRL

FIND ME IN SIX - TRANQUILITY

IN SOLITUDE

IT MATTERS NOT

KISS THE RAIN

LIFE IS A DANCE

LIKE CHASING RAIN

SONG FOR MY LOVE, MY SWEET

STAR-CROSSED FOR LOVE OF DAY, FOR THE LOVE OF NIGHT

THE SIX - MY HEART SINGS OUT

WHAT LOVE IS

WINTER BLUES

WORDS NEVER SPOKEN

JEAN BAPTISTE AND SISTINE

1 - AMIDST THE STORM OF SOUND

2 - INSIDE THIS GUST OF WIND

3 - KINDRED SOULS

4 - ON LOVE

5 - SISTINE AND JEAN-BAPTISTE

6 - THANK YOU

A HOME SWEET HOME

AT LONG DAY'S END, OUR THOUGHTS MAY STRAY TO WHERE WE LONG TO WEND OUR WAY- A PEACEFUL PLACE WHERE WE DISMISS ALL THINGS IN LIFE THAT ARE AMISS, AND NONE ARE WONT TO CAUSE DISMAY.

OUR FOOTSTEPS HASTEN US TO THIS: THE WARMTH OF HEARTH, THE WELCOME KISS. FOR THOSE LESS FORTUNATE I PRAY A HOME SWEET HOME THEY'LL FIND ONE DAY.

A TALE OF FIRE AND ICE

PART I: ICE

HE SHINES LIKE SILVER MIDNIGHT MOON - COOL MARBLE STATUE,
THIS TYCOON. AND THOUGH HE MAKES THE LADIES SWOON, OF ICE
HE'S HEWN.; OF ICE HE'S HEWN.

HE'S POKER-FACED AND CAN DECEIVE COMPETITORS AND CAN ACHIEVE
MOST ANYTHING, BUT CAN'T CONCEIVE OF GENEVIEVE, OF GENEVIEVE.

LIKE NEPTUNE, DISTANT FROM THE SUN - RELATIONSHIPS HE CHOSE TO SHUN.
HE THOUGHT THE SEARCH FOR LOVE WAS DONE. HE HAS NO ONE; HE HAS NO ONE.

NOW LOVE'S ALLURE HAS COME HIS WAY. WHAT WILL HE DO? WHAT WILL HE SAY?
WILL HE GRAB HOLD, BEG LOVE TO STAY, OR LET IT STRAY? OR LET IT STRAY?

PART II: FIRE

THIS DRAGONESS DISGUISED IN LACE - PASSION'S FLOWER WITH ANGEL'S FACE,
PRECISELY PICKS THE TIME AND PLACE EACH DREAM TO CHASE,
EACH DREAM TO CHASE.

LIKE INK THE COLOR RED, SHE STAINS THE HEARTS OF THOSE WHOSE LOVE SHE
DRAINS, AND THEN SHE LEAVES WHEN NAUGHT REMAINS NO LUST SHE FEIGNS;
NO LUST SHE FEIGNS.

AND NOW THERE'S ONE WHO WOULD SUFFICE. FOR HIM ALONE, SHE'D
SACRIFICE HER EVERYTHING, SO HE OF ICE SHE MUST
ENTICE, SHE MUST ENTICE.

SO GENEVIEVE NOW STRIKES THE FLAME. WILL MAN OF ICE HIS
LOVE PROCLAIM? BENEATH HER FIRE AND HIS COLD FRAME,
THEY'RE BOTH THE SAME. THEY'RE BOTH THE SAME.

A TRIBUTE TO A STAR

ON YOU THE ANGELS DID BESTOW A GLOW YOUR FRIENDS
WOULD COME TO KNOW AS STAR-SHINE!

FOR EVEN STARS CANNOT OUTSHINE YOUR COUNTENANCE.
IT'S AS DIVINE AS STARLIGHT.

OH, HOW YOU HUSH THOSE STARS, MY DEAR, FROM BRIGHTLY
SHINING WHEN YOU'RE NEAR; THEY'RE STAR-STRUCK.

I TOO AM STRICKEN BY YOUR SIGHT.
I'D LOVE TO BE WITH YOU ALL NIGHT
TO STAR-GAZE.

SHINE ON, SWEET MAN, BUT DO NOT BURN TOO LONG OR STRONGLY;
STARS MIGHT TURN TO STARDUST!

AT THE END OF THE RAINBOW

AT THE END OF THE RAINBOW, DREAMS UNFOLD.
AND SOME PEOPLE SAY THERE IS A POT OF GOLD.

HOW WELL I RECALL A RAINBOW ONE DAY
THAT SHONE IN THE SKY WHEN A STORM WENT AWAY.

RAIN PELTED MY CAR; I FELT SO AFRAID.
BUT AS I NEARED HOME, IT STARTED TO FADE.
THE SKY, ONCE SO DARK, GREW MORE AND MORE BLUE.
I THRILLED NEXT TO SEE A RAINBOW ARCH THROUGH!

IT BENT TOWARD THE MOUNTAINS, SO BEAUTIFUL, A PEACE AND GREAT
JOY WELLED UP IN MY SOUL.
NO POT OF GOLD AT ITS END DID I SEE,
BUT STILL THERE WAS GOLD AND IT BECKONED TO ME.

THE MOUNTAINS WERE GILDED WITH A BRIGHT GLEAM.
THIS IS THE MAGIC THAT MAKES POETS DREAM!

WHEN I GOT HOME, I TOOK PAPER AND PEN
AND WROTE OF THAT BEAUTY, GOD'S PROMISE TO MEN.

AGAIN I RECALL HOW MY SOUL LIFTED.
AT THE RAINBOW'S END, GOD'S LOVE IS GIFTED.

CINDER GIRL

AN EMBER SPARKED WILL SOFTLY GLOW,
AND FED BY FUEL, WILL GROW AND GROW.
I ONCE WAS CINDER, SPARKED BY YOU, FIRST TIMID. . .
TILL THE FLAMES THEN GREW.

AND SO OUR START WAS TOUCH OF DAWN,
WITH AMBER HUE, FOR I WAS DRAWN.
TO EYES SO WELCOMING AND WARM,
I NEVER GUESSED YOU'D DO ME HARM.

LIKE MORNING GLORY, LOVE IN JUNE,
THE RAPTURE OF MID-AFTERNOON,
ROMANCE OF WHICH THE ANCIENTS WROTE,
OUR PASSION HAD NO ANTIDOTE.

AND WITH THE DUSK, THOUGH SCARLET TINGED,
OUR LOVE BEGAN TO COME UNHINGED,
FOR CLOUDS ARRIVED, WHICH FILLED YOUR EYES,
EXTINGUISHING BRIGHT TWILIGHT SKIES.

WITH COLD OF NIGHT CAME SHADOWS' PALL,
AND I COULD NOT TEAR DOWN YOUR WALL.
BY MIDNIGHT'S HOUR, THE FIRE WAS DEAD,
MERE ASHES SMOLDERED IN ITS STEAD.

YOU LEFT, AND SHOULD YOU REAPPEAR,
I'VE VOWED TO SHUN YOU. NOW I FEAR
THE VERY THING FOR WHICH I YEARN -
ONE TOUCH. . . AND THEN AGAIN - TO BURN.

FIND ME IN SIX – TRANQUILITY

FIND ME WHERE THE SUMMER BREEZE IS SIGHING.
THERE TIME FLOATS ME IN ITS ENDLESS SEA.
ENGULFED AM I - BY SWEET TRANQUILITY.
ON A LOFTY ESPLANADE, GULLS FLYING
ARE TRAILING CLOUDS THROUGH AZURE, WHEELING FREE.
SUN FLASHES GOLD ITS GRIN! THERE YOU'LL FIND ME.

IN SOLITUDE

IN SOLITUDE, I WATCH THE CLEAR BLUE SKY. LEAVES FLUTTER ON THE
GRAND MAJESTIC OAK BENEATH WHICH I AM SITTING;
SWALLOWS FLY AROUND ME, SWOOPING!

NOW I HEAR A CROAK - A SOUND THAT I AM SURE I'D NEVER
HEAR IF I WERE ON A BUSY CITY STREET. I STAND AND WALK AROUND.
THE SOUND IS NEAR. THE FEELING THAT I GET IS RATHER SWEET WHEN
FINALLY I SPOT THERE ON THE POND THE TINY FROG THAT'S SERENADING ME.

CROPS RIPPLING IN THE BREEZE I SEE BEYOND MY SHADED SPOT. I SOON
MUST LEAVE MY TREE. RED SUNSET I WILL WATCH BEFORE I CREEP IN
QUIET OF THE NIGHT BACK HOME TO SLEEP!

IT MATTERS NOT

IT HOVERS HERE, A MOON OPAQUE,
OBSCURING MOUNTAIN TRAILS I TAKE.
NO OTHER LIVING THINGS APPEAR.
A MOON OPAQUE. . . IT HOVERS HERE.

I FOLLOW ON ALONG A LEDGE;
BELOW A SWIRLING RIVER'S EDGE.
IN FRONT OF ME, THE CANYON'S YAWN.
ALONG A LEDGE, I FOLLOW ON.

I SEE NO HUE WHEN FOG CONGEALS.
OH, DOOM OF ONE WHO NO MORE FEELS!
THE MOON HAS FLED, AS SO HAVE YOU.
WHEN FOG CONGEALS, I SEE NO HUE.

NOW ALL IS DIM; IT MATTERS NOT.
MY DEAR ONE'S HEART I HAVE NOT GOT.
NO USE IN LIVING WITHOUT HIM.
IT MATTERS NOT. NOW ALL IS DIM.

AT PEACE I'LL BE IF I SHOULD FALL
TO MURKY WATER FROM THIS WALL.
OH, YAWNING CANYON, SWALLOW ME.
IF I SHOULD FALL, AT PEACE I'LL BE.

KISS THE RAIN

I STAND HERE BY THE LAKESHORE, AND I SMELL FRESH
HONEYSUCKLE AS I KISS THE RAIN. A MEMORY THAT I CANNOT
CURTAIL WAFTS BITTER SWEETLY TO ME, AND AGAIN IT'S MAY. . .
THE NIGHT YOU CAME TO ME BY MOONLIGHT.
THE AIR WAS PERMEATED BY PERFUME
FROM BLOSSOMS COLORED INNOCENTLY WHITE.

BUT NOW IT'S SUMMER; YELLOW IS EACH
BLOOM. WHEN PLUMP UPON THE VINES, SWEET BERRIES,
RED, WILL BE SWOOPED UP BY BIRDS AND
CARRIED AWAY. I STOOP TO TOUCH A STEM.
HOW SOON HAS FLED MY FLOWERED
YOUTH, AND NOW THIS DAY CHILLED GREY, I BOW IN
DOWNPOUR LIKE THE VINES BENT LOW WHILE RAINDROPS TURN
TO TEARS AND - GLISTENING - FLOW.

LIFE IS A DANCE

LIFE IS A DANCE WE WERE ALL BORN TO DO. THE STYLES TO CHOOSE FROM ARE MORE THAN A FEW! SOME CHOOSE SIMPLE TWO-STEP; SOME MOVE WITH FLAIR. SOME SLOW DANCE; SOME BREAK DANCE, DEVIL-MAY-CARE! SOME FREE STYLE, WHILE OTHERS JUST DANCE ON CUE.

SOME TANGO WITH ZEST; SOME SHUFFLE SOFT-SHOE. OTHERS GLIDE EASILY, WALTZING ON THROUGH. SOME CHANGE THEIR PARTNERS; SOME STAY ONE PAIR. LIFE IS A DANCE.

YOU START WITH THE STYLES IN YOUR OWN MILIEU, THEN GROW AS YOU ADD ON NEW MOVES YOU VIEW. YOU'LL STUMBLE, BUT SOMETIMES DANCE ON SWEET AIR! JUST KEEP THE BEAT; TRY NEW STEPS IF YOU DARE, FOR WHERE YOU END UP IS ALL UP TO YOU... LIFE IS A DANCE!

LIKE CLEANSING RAIN

SUCH CONTEMPLATING THAT THE POETS DO.
THEY SING OF GOD, OUR SPIRITS TO RENEW.

WITH MOTHER NATURE OFTEN THEY'RE IN TUNE
AND OFFER UP THEIR VERSE TO SUN AND MOON.

THEY PRAISE THE SUNSET OVER A BLUE LAKE
WHILE PONDERING MAN'S PURPOSE, AND THEY ACHE...
THEY ACHE FOR ALL THAT EARTH CAN NEVER BE,
FOR DREAMS THEY'VE LOST, AND FOR HUMANITY.

AND WHEN THEY ACHE, THEIR WORDS ARE FILLED WITH PAIN
WHICH POUR OUT FROM THEIR SOUL LIKE CLEANSING RAIN!

SONG FOR MY LOVE, MY SWEET

AT LAST YOU'VE COME FOR ME, MY LOVE, MY SWEET! YOU'VE COME THROUGH TRANQUIL WOODLAND, WITH THE BREEZE, ALONG THAT PATH WHERE ONCE WE USED TO MEET AND WITH THE SUNLIGHT STREAMING THROUGH THE TREES!

WITH PASSION IN YOUR EYES AND WINGS FOR FEET, YOU'VE COME FOR ME, AND ALL MY ANGUISH FLEES. YOU ARE SO NEAR, I HEAR YOUR WILD HEART BEAT. YOU'VE COME FOR ME, MY OWN WILD HEART TO SEIZE.

ALAS! THE WOODS HAVE VANISHED WITH THE GLEAM OF MY WAKING DAWN. IT WAS BUT A DREAM.

STAR-CROSSED – FOR LOVE OF DAY, FOR THE LOVE OF NIGHT

IN SHADOWS' VEILS, AT END OF NIGHT, SWEET MOON REMOVES HER
MODEST LIGHT AND SOFTLY, YET AGAIN, EXHALES - AT END
OF NIGHT, IN SHADOWS' VEILS.

AS SHE DEPARTS, HER LOVE'S RELEASED TO CLIMB THE STAIRWAY
TO THE EAST. THEY CANNOT MEET TO SHARE THEIR HEARTS.
HER LOVE'S RELEASED AS SHE DEPARTS.

SHE WATCHES HIM WHILE HID FROM VIEW, THE WAY HE KISSES
MORNING'S DEW, AND SEES GOLD RAYS SPILL FROM HIS RIM.
WHILE HID FROM VIEW, SHE WATCHES HIM.

SAD MOON, ALONE FOR CENTURIES, WITH AWE HAS WATCHED
SUN LEAVE, CERISE. WHILE SHE, AFAR. . . HOW COLD SHE'S GROWN!
FOR CENTURIES, SAD MOON ALONE.

SHE TAKES HIS PLACE SO HE MAY REST. AND THOUGH FORLORN,
SHE'S ALWAYS DRESSED IN LACE, FOR LUNA HAS GREAT GRACE. SO HE MAY
REST, SHE TAKES HIS PLACE.

FOR LOVE OF NIGHT, FOR LOVE OF DAY, SHE CAN'T IMPLORE HIM THAT HE SWAY
FROM COURSE. TO BE APART'S THEIR PLIGHT.
FOR LOVE OF DAY, FOR LOVE OF NIGHT.

THE SIX - MY HEART SINGS OUT

TO HEAR THE SURF OR TRILL OF SPRING'S NEW BIRDS;
A CAT'S SOFT PURR OR STRONG AND STIRRING WORDS;
ENDEARMENTS WHISPERED; SONGS SO CUTE I GRIN,
MY HEART SINGS OUT AS JOY WELLS UP WITHIN.

TO SEE THE SUN FALL, GORGEOUS ON THE SEA;
ANUNEXPECTED RAINBOW OVER ME;
A MOVING SCENE; GLAD FACES OF MY KIN,
MY HEART SINGS OUT AS JOY WELLS UP WITHIN.

TO SMELL A ROSE; SWEET LAVENDER IN BLOOM;
POPCORN AT THE MOVIES; FAVORITE PERFUME;
AROMA OF MOM'S COOKING
ONCE AGAIN, MY HEART SINGS OUT AS JOY WELLS UP WITHIN.

TO TASTE DELICIOUS FOOD WHEN OUT TO DINE;
ICE CREAM ON MY TONGUE; A LOVER'S MOUTH ON MINE;
COLD DRINKS; DESSERTS AS CHOCOLATY AS SIN,
MY HEART SINGS OUT AS JOYS WELLS UP WITHIN.

TO FEEL A GENTLE RAIN; SNOWFLAKES ON MY NOSE;
OCEAN'S BREEZE; THE TIDES; THE SAND BETWEEN MY TOES;
SUN'S WARMTH; THE HEAT OF PASSION ON MY SKIN,
MY HEART SINGS OUT AS JOY WELLS UP WITHIN.

TO FEEL INSIDE ME SUCH A HAPPY GLOW
IT RADIATES TO EVERYONE I KNOW;
THE LOVE THAT LETS ME KNOW LIFE IS WIN-WIN,
MY HEART SINGS OUT AS JOY WELLS UP WITHIN.

WHAT LOVE IS

WHEN LOVE COMES POUNDING ON A DRUM,
IT COMES ON FAST AND HARD AND STRONG
UNTIL TWO HEARTS IN SYNCH BEAT PASSION'S SONG.

SOMETIMES LOVE COMES CLANGING DOWN THE TRACKS.
IT CLASHES OR IT CLAMORS TO BE HEARD,
SO AT ITS CROSSING, MEANING IS OBSCURED.

OTHER TIMES, LOVE LURKS OR IT ATTACKS.
UNREQUITED, LOVE CAN PIERCE OR BURN
UNTIL ITS VENTRICLE TURNS INTO BLACK.

AND THEN ARE TIMES LOVE GENTLY CLIMBS
OR EASES SURE-FOOTED TO ONE'S DOOR
OR SWEETLY SEEPS AND SATURATES THE SOUL.

IT'S STRONG AND YET IT'S SOFT.
IT DOESN'T STING OR SNIP. IT LISTENS
AND REVERBERATES THE WHISPERS OF THE HEART.

WINTER BLUES

ANOTHER YEAR HAS COME - CHILLINGLY - AND MORE
CHILLINGLY FOR ME THAN IN DECADES HERETOFORE.
I WATCH IT RANTING FROM MY WINDOW AS I RECALL...

THE YEAR ALREADY PAST HAD TUGGED ME FROM THOSE
TAME AND TOASTY DAYS WHEN I LAY FACE UP TO SUN DREAMING
THAT MY SUMMER WOULD NEVER END. IT BROUGHT ME TO THIS
WINTER WHEN IT WITHERED UP AND DIED, BUT HALF A CENTURY
AND MORE OF MEMORIES HAD FALLEN FOR ME BY NOW. LIKE
PRETTY CRYSTAL FLAKES THEY FELL, DRIFTING THROUGH MY MIND –
PLACES, EVENTS AND PEOPLE.

OH, THOSE PEOPLE I LOOKED UP TO IN MY YOUTH - FALLEN AS THE
SNOW! HOW MANY PRETTY SNOW FLAKES HAVE MELTED NOW AWAY?
ONLY MY MEMORIES OF THEM REMAIN... MEMORIES
NOW PILED UP LIKE SNOWDRIFTS IN MY BRAIN.
YES, THE NEWBORN YEAR HAS ARRIVED. JUST ONE MONTH OLD AND
ALREADY, IT HAS LOST ITS CRAWL. THIS INFANT'S AGING PROCESS
PARALLELS, ON THE LARGER SCALE, THAT FLEETING SPAN OF TIME KNOWN
AS LIFE - A TIME THAT ALL THE LIVING UNDERGO.

THE NEW YEAR CARRIES ON (AS MUST WE ALL) TO SOON
COMPLETE ITS CYCLE. LET IT BLUSTER. LET IT WAIL. LET IT RATTLE
AT MY DOOR, FOR SOON ENOUGH, ALL SIGNS OF IT WILL CEASE.

WORDS I'VE NEVER SPOKEN

WORDS I'VE NEVER SPOKEN ARE THOSE I'LL NEVER WRITE,
LIKE WORDS THAT MIGHT RECALL THE GLOW I FELT ONE NIGHT...

ONE CHOICE LIFETIME'S FRAGMENT I TOOK FOR PARADISE...
A TIME FOR WHICH MY MEMORY ALONE CANNOT SUFFICE.

ONE SUMMER'S WHISPERED END... YOUR FEEL, YOUR TOUCH,
YOUR SCENT, YOUR LASHES ON MY CHEEK, THE PURE ENRAPTUREMENT...

YOUR HANDS AND HAIR LIKE SILK, YOUR PAUSE TO GAZE ON ME -
THEY SEEM MORE AN ILLUSION NOW THAN PAST REALITY.

WORDS I'VE NEVER SPOKEN ARE THOSE I'LL NEVER WRITE,
LIKE WORDS THAT MIGHT RECALL THE GLOW I FELT ONE NIGHT...

NO WORDS CAN BRING TO LIFE THE FLEETING GHOST OF YOU.
YOU HAUNT MY EMPTY HOURS; THERE'S NOTHING I CAN DO,

FOR IF YOU THINK OF ME, I GUESS I'LL NEVER KNOW.
AND HOW YOU MADE ME THRILL NO WORDS CAN EVER SHOW.

WORDS I'VE NEVER SPOKEN ARE THOSE I'LL NEVER WRITE,
LIKE WORDS THAT MIGHT RECALL THE GLOW I FELT ONE NIGHT...

JEAN-BAPTISTE AND SISTINE

POEM #1: AMIDST THE STORM OF SOUND

HE:

THE DISSONANCE OF HUMANS' SOUND -
THEIR NEVER-CEASING MILLING ALL AROUND,
THEIR BLARING HORNS AND WORKERS IN THE STREET
POUND POUND POUNDING ON THE GROUND.
CLOUDS SO GRAY AND CLUMPED TOGETHER
UGLY AS LONDON'S SOMETIMES(OFTIMES?) FOGGY WEATHER!
HANGING OVER ME, THEY ARE A SHROUD.

AND THEN, AMIDST ALL THIS, I SEE YOU HERE.
A WOMAN, LIKE A NYMPH
WHO WATCHES ME AS IF FROM INSIDE A SNOW GLOBE.
IF I SHAKE THE GLOBE, ALL THE NOISE WILL DISAPPEAR.
THE STORM OF SOUND THAT ONCE RAINED IN MY EAR
WILL   ALL   FADE   AWAY.
YOU ARE NOT OF THIS UNHOLY SPHERE.
OH NYMPH MOST RARE, YOU BECKON ME WITH EYES THAT I ALREADY KNOW!
MY SWEET SISTINE.

SHE:

JEAN, JEAN-BAPTISTE, I SEE YOU TOO.
YOU WHO ARE THE BREATH OF WIND
WITH WHICH I LONG TO DANCE.
A BREATH OF WIND AS FRESH AS SNOW PRISTINE.

POEM #2: INSIDE THIS GUST OF WIND

HE:

AH, SHE LOOKS SO WELL PUT TOGETHER.
HAIR UP IN A BUN.
SHE'S ALL DRESSED FOR BUSINESS.
BUT TAKE A CLOSER LOOK -
BEYOND WHAT SHE IS READING IN HER BOOK...

I BET IF SHE SHOULD GRACE ME WITH A SMILE,
TEETH WHITE AND PERFECT SHE WOULD REVEAL.
OH, TO SEE HER SMILE
IF ONLY FOR A WHILE!

HER HAND... IT TREMBLES.
OH, TO CLASP THAT PRECIOUS HAND,
TO FEEL HER FINGERS INTERTWINED WITH MINE

SHE:

THOSE EYES NOW MEETING MINE.
ARE THEY BLUE OR GREY? I CAN'T REALLY SAY.
BUT OH, THEY ARE DIVINE!

SUITED AND BOOTED,
HE LOOKS DRESSED FOR BUSINESS,
BUT WHAT REALLY LIES
BEHIND HIS SOFT EYES?

HOW IS IT THAT I FIND MYSELF LONGING
TO TOUCH HIS FACE SO FAIR?
AND HIS HAIR
TOUSLED BY THE WIND -
HOW I WISH TO REACH OUT TO HIM,
HIS GOLDEN HAIR TO SMOOTHE.

INSIDE THIS GUST OF WIND IS ONLY HIM,
AND I AM SOOTHED.

POEM #3 - KINDRED SOULS

HE:

MY MIND WAS IN A WHIRL...WHO WAS THIS GIRL? WHO IS THIS GIRL?
I'VE FOLLOWED HER AND WHERE I NEXT WILL GO
I DO NOT EVEN REALLY NEED TO KNOW!
SHE SMASHED MY PHONE ALONG WITH HERS! IMAGINE THAT.
AND I, SO OFTEN STAID, FOLLOWED SUIT, DOING IT WITH GLEE!
IN LETTING GO, I'M FEELING FREE,
AND FREEDOM'S OTHER NAME I'M LEARNING, IS TRANQUILITY.

FOR WE CAN BE IN LONDON FIELDS
WITH PEOPLE ALL AROUND US ON THE RUN,
I ONLY NEED TO BE WITH HER
AND WATCH HER SWIRL A DANDELION IN THE SUN!
MY GOLDEN PETAL IN THE SUN THIS WOMAN HAS BECOME.
SISTINE, SISTINE - YOU HOLD YOUR ARMS OUT WIDE.
A GENTLE TOUCH FROM YOU, INTO YOUR SOUL I GLIDE.

SHE:

IN SPITE OF EVERYTHING WITH WHICH I'M DEALING,
HOW STRANGELY WONDERFUL I NOW AM FEELING.
TO FIND THIS MAN IN ALL OF (LONDON), SEEMING SO LIKE ME.
THAT DEEP CONNECTION - INSTANT CHEMISTY!
A STRANGER, YET A KINDRED SPIRIT IN HIS EYES I SEE.

I LEAD, HE FOLLOWS. HE DOESN'T QUESTION ANYTHING I SAY.
HIS FINGERS LIGHTLY GRAZE MY SKIN, OUR FINGERS INTERLOCK...
KINDRED SOULS, WE SLEEP INSIDE THE CAR,
THEN WAKEN TO EMBRACE A BRAND NEW DAY.
WE DRIVE, WE WALK.
WE HAVE NO NEED TO TALK.
WE SIMPLY FEEL.
JEAN-BAPTISTE, THERE ARE NO WORDS TO SAY...

POEM #4 – ON LOVE

HE:

LIKE MULTI-COLORED FLOWERS IN THE WILD,
LOVE BLOSSOMS IN A VAST ARRAY OF HUES.
WHAT JOY THE MOTHER FEELS WHEN HER SWEET CHILD
INSIDE HER ARMS LOOKS UP AT HER AND COOS.

HOW NECESSARY IS THIS FIRST DEEP BOND TO EVERYONE!
IT NOURISHES THE HEART,
FOR AS THE CHILD MATURES, HE SEES BEYOND
FAMILIAL BONDS. LOVE'S LANDSCAPE IS OUR ART.

IN SOFT OR BRILLIANT COLORS WE CHOOSE TO PAINT
THE DIFFERENT FORMS OF IT THAT WE MAY FIND,
AND LOVE MAY BE A HARLOT OR A SAINT,
BUT WHEN IT'S TRUE, IT CHOOSES TO BE BLIND!

SHE:

YES, LOVE IS EVEN TRUER WHEN WE SEE
PAST ANY FRAILITIES; ACCEPTING ALL!
OUR DOG AND CAT FRIENDS DO NOT MIND IF WE HAVE FLAWS!
REAL LOVE MEANS BREAKING DOWN THE WALLS.

THE FRIENDS WHO WE HOLD CLOSE TO US ARE THOSE
WHO LOVE US AS WE ARE, BUT THERE IS TOO
A LOVE THAT HAPPENS SUDDENLY AND GROWS -
DAWN OVERTAKING NIGHT AS IT BURSTS THROUGH!

LOVE'S EVERY COLOR OUGHT TO OFFER PEACE.
LIKE LOVE OF SWEETHEARTS OR OF MAN AND WIFE,
BUT EVEN THOSE DESIRES WE KNOW MUST CEASE
ARE UNEXPECTED SUN-BURSTS IN OUR LIFE!

POEM #5– SISTINE AND JEAN-BAPTISTE

HE:

I DIDN'T KNOW SISTINE AT ALL
WHEN FIRST I SAW HER READING ON THE PARK BENCH.
HOW CAN I EXPLAIN ALL THAT SHE'S BEEN
AND WHAT MY SIX DAYS OF SISTINE HAVE MEANT?

HER GRACEFUL HANDS, LONG HAIR, AND SOULFUL EYES -
VERY SOON I WOULD COME TO REALIZE
THAT BEYOND THE BEAUTY OF HER SKIN
IS SOMETHING EVEN LOVELIER WITHIN.

I FOLLOWED HER THROUGH BRICK LANE AND EAST LONDON MARKETS.
SHE PICKED OUT CLOTHING BEAUTIFUL AND BRIGHT.
SHE'S UNPREDICTABLE, SPONTANEOUS AND BRAVE.
I'D FOLLOW HER INTO THE DARKEST SHADOWS OF THE NIGHT.

HOW COULD I NOT FOLLOW? AN ANGEL IS SISTINE.
HOW CALM SHE IS. HOW COMFORTING.
ON THE OTHER SIDE OF MY OWN FENCE,
SHE'S THE GRASS MOST COVETED AND GREEN.

AND YET SHE IS A WOMAN WITH A PAST, WITH FAMILY!
CONFLICTED, SHE HAD GREAT PAIN I WANTED TO ALLAY.
I KNEW BY THE END OF OUR SIX DAYS, IT WOULD NOT LAST.
BUT BLESSED WAS I TO COMFORT HER AS IN MY ARMS SHE LAY.

SHE:

OH, HOW I LOVED MY TIME WITH JEAN-BAPTISTE!
AN ATTRACTIVE MAN WELL SUITED I FIRST COULD SEE-
THE EPITOME OF SOMEONE REGIMENTED IN HIS THINKING,
BUT IN THE DIN OF CITY LIFE, JEAN-BAPTISTE WAS SINKING.

DESPITE ALL THAT, I COULD SEE AT LEAST
THERE WAS A SPARK IN HIM, AND IN A WHILE,
THIS MAN ONCE QUIET AND WITHDRAWN,
BROUGHT MY SOUL TO LIFE AND MADE ME SMILE.
HOW EAGERLY I SAW HIM THEN EMBRACE THE AMBER DAWN.

HE LOOKED ABOUT FOR SOMETHING THAT HE COULD NOT FIND,
BUT IT WAS THERE BEFORE HIM ALL THE TIME.
WITH FREEDOM AND A NEWLY BORN TRANQUILITY,
HE FOUND HIS OWN TRUTHS WITH HIS CLEVER MIND.

HOW FINE A MIND IT IS - BEHIND THOSE SLATE BLUE EYES!
DANCING THROUGH THE STREETS IN OUR MORNING GLORY DAYS
TILL DUSK BLED CRIMSON, THEN AGAIN WAKING TO EACH SUNRISE,
TOGETHER, IN THIS FLEET AND PRECIOUS PHASE,

WE WERE MEANT TO BE!

HOW TRUSTING AND HOW SWEET IS HE -
THIS KINDRED SPIRIT, WHO LIKE ME,
NEEDED COMFORT IN OUR MUTUAL
SEARCH FOR CLARITY!

POEM #6 – THANK YOU

HE:

SISTINE, I THANK YOU FOR YOUR GIFTS TO ME.
I NEEDED SOME ASSURANCE, AND WITH THAT WAY UNIQUELY YOURS,
YOU SHOWED ME WHAT TO DO.
YOU HELPED ME TO ESCAPE PREDICTABILITY.
IF NOT FOR YOU, I'D NOT HAVE BEEN SET FREE.
MY SIMPLE GIFT, SISTINE, IS A RED ROSE FOR YOU.

SHE:

DEAR MAN, WITH EYES AS WARM AS THOSE FEW DAYS IN MAY
IN WHICH WE WERE TOGETHER -
I NEEDED COMFORT; IN YOUR TRUSTING WAY,
YOU FOLLOWED WHERE I LED, UNQUESTIONINGLY.
I THANK YOU, JEAN BAPTISTE,
FOR LAYING BARE YOUR SOUL TO ME.
YOUR SMILE, YOUR GENTLE TOUCH . . .
ALL HAVE MEANT SO VERY MUCH.

HE:

WE BARED THE PUREST PART OF OURSELVES TO ONE ANOTHER.
WHATEVER HAPPENS IN MY FUTURE, THERE WILL BE NO OTHER
WHOM I WILL LOOK BACK ON WITH SUCH TENDERNESS.
THANK YOU FOR THE COMFORT IN YOUR SWEET CARESS.
YOU HELPED ME SEE THAT THE PROBLEMS FROM WHICH I RAN
WERE NOT SO DIFFICULT TO SOLVE.
THANKS TO YOU, I'M NOW A STRONGER MAN.

SHE:

YOU DIDN'T TRY TO FIX ME, JEAN-BAPTISTE.
YOU LET ME FALL INTO YOUR ARMS, RELEASING PAIN.
HOW PATIENT YOU HAVE BEEN, HOW VERY SWEET.
A STRONGER WOMAN I HAVE NOW BECOME.
SINCE KNOWING YOU, I'VE LEARNED TO KISS THE RAIN.
AND IN MY DREAMS, JEAN-BAPTISTE, I'LL SEE YOU AGAIN.

TOGETHER:

I NEEDED YOU; YOU NEEDED ME,
AND WHEN I SAW YOUR FACE,
TRANQUILITY ENVELOPED ME.
THANK YOU, DEAR, FOR BEING THERE.
THANK YOU FOR YOUR GRACE.

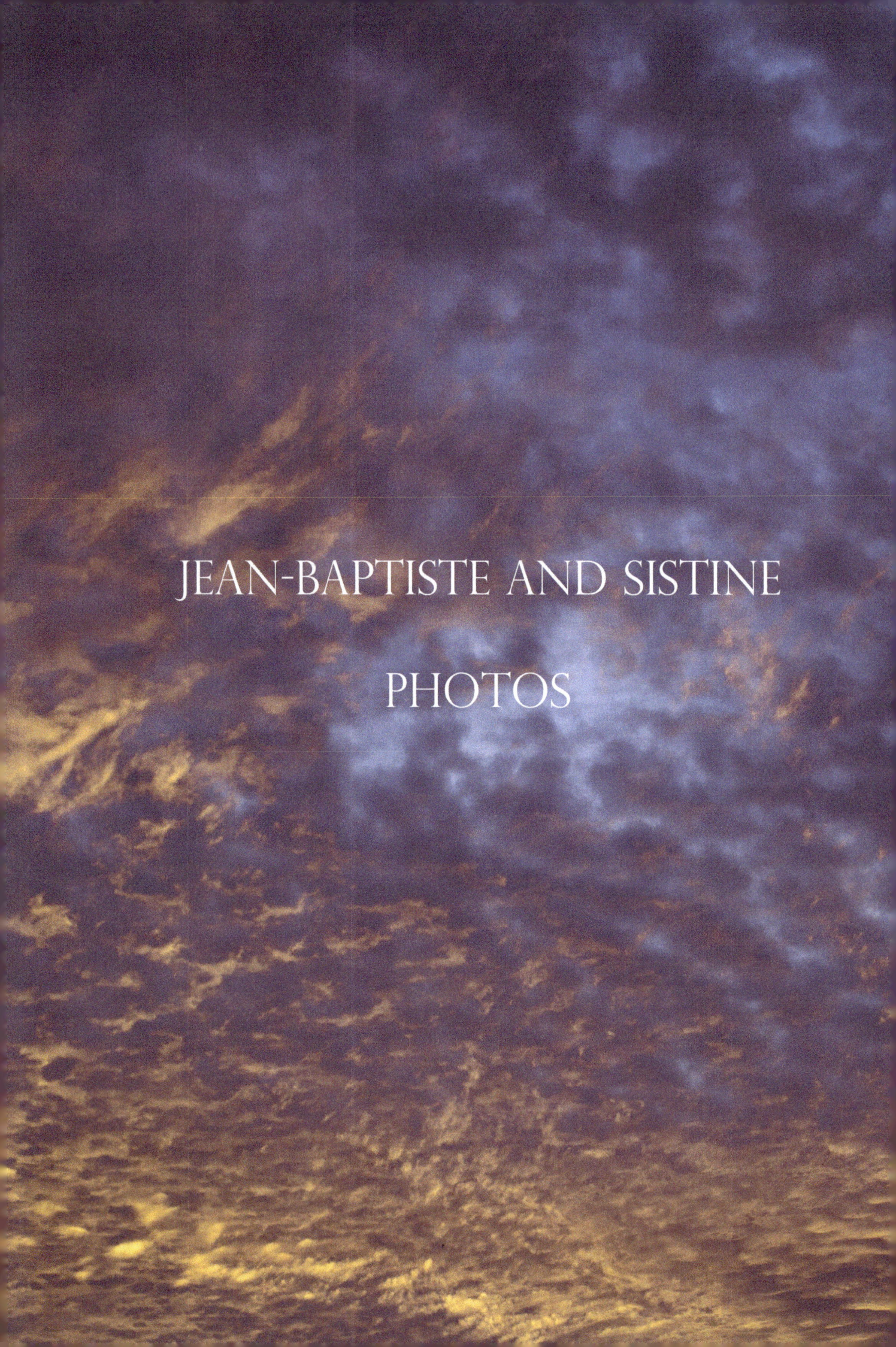

JEAN-BAPTISTE AND SISTINE

PHOTOS

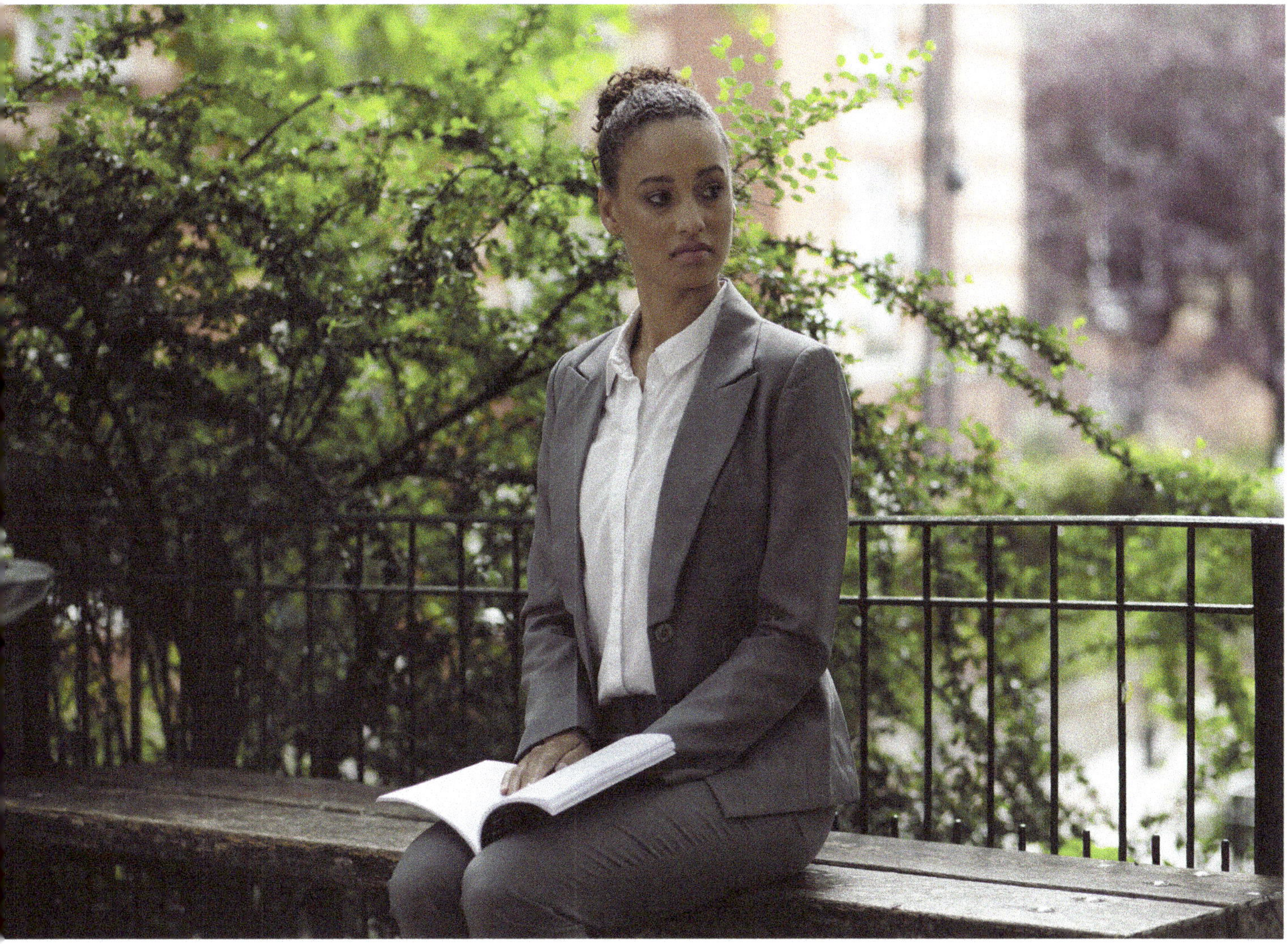

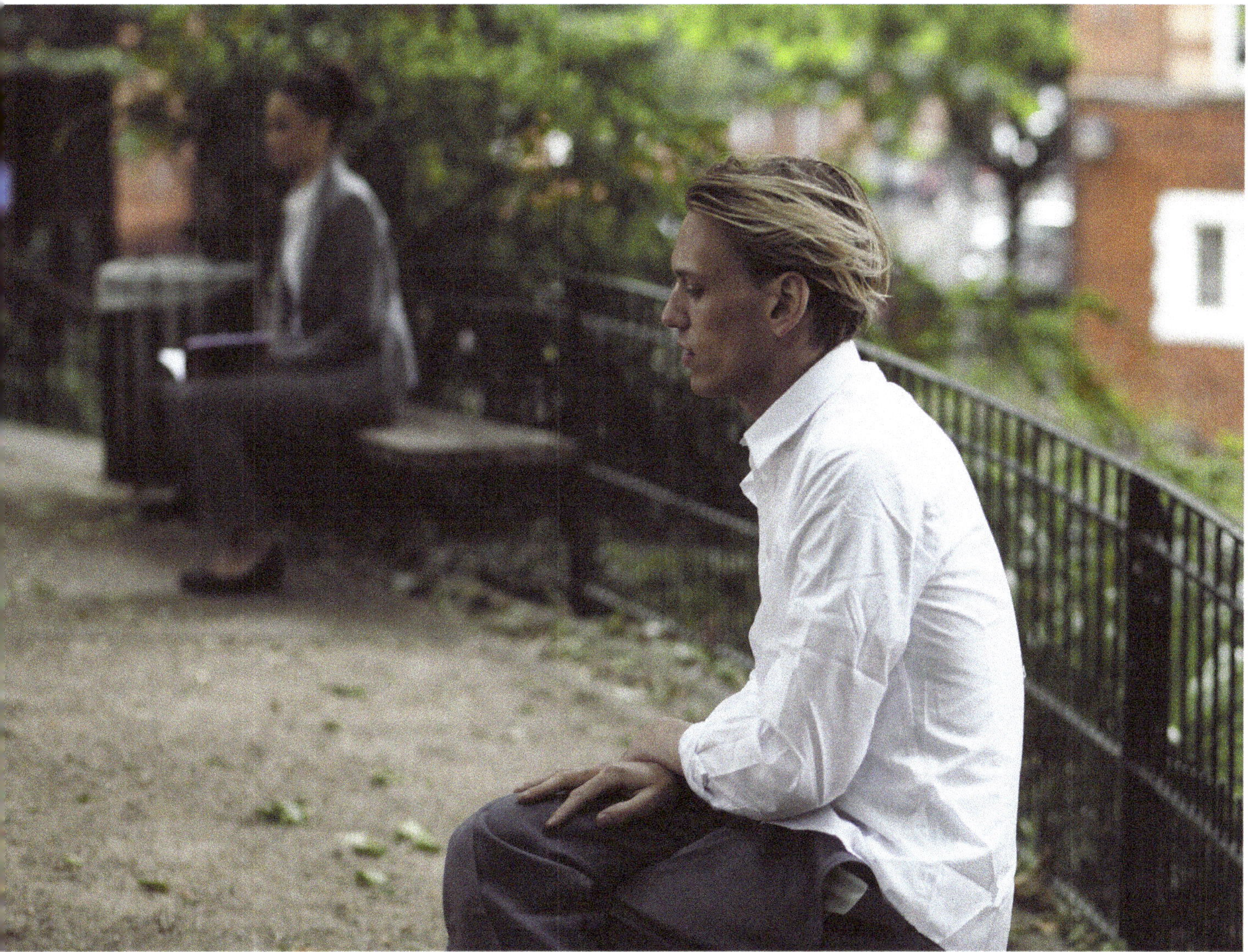

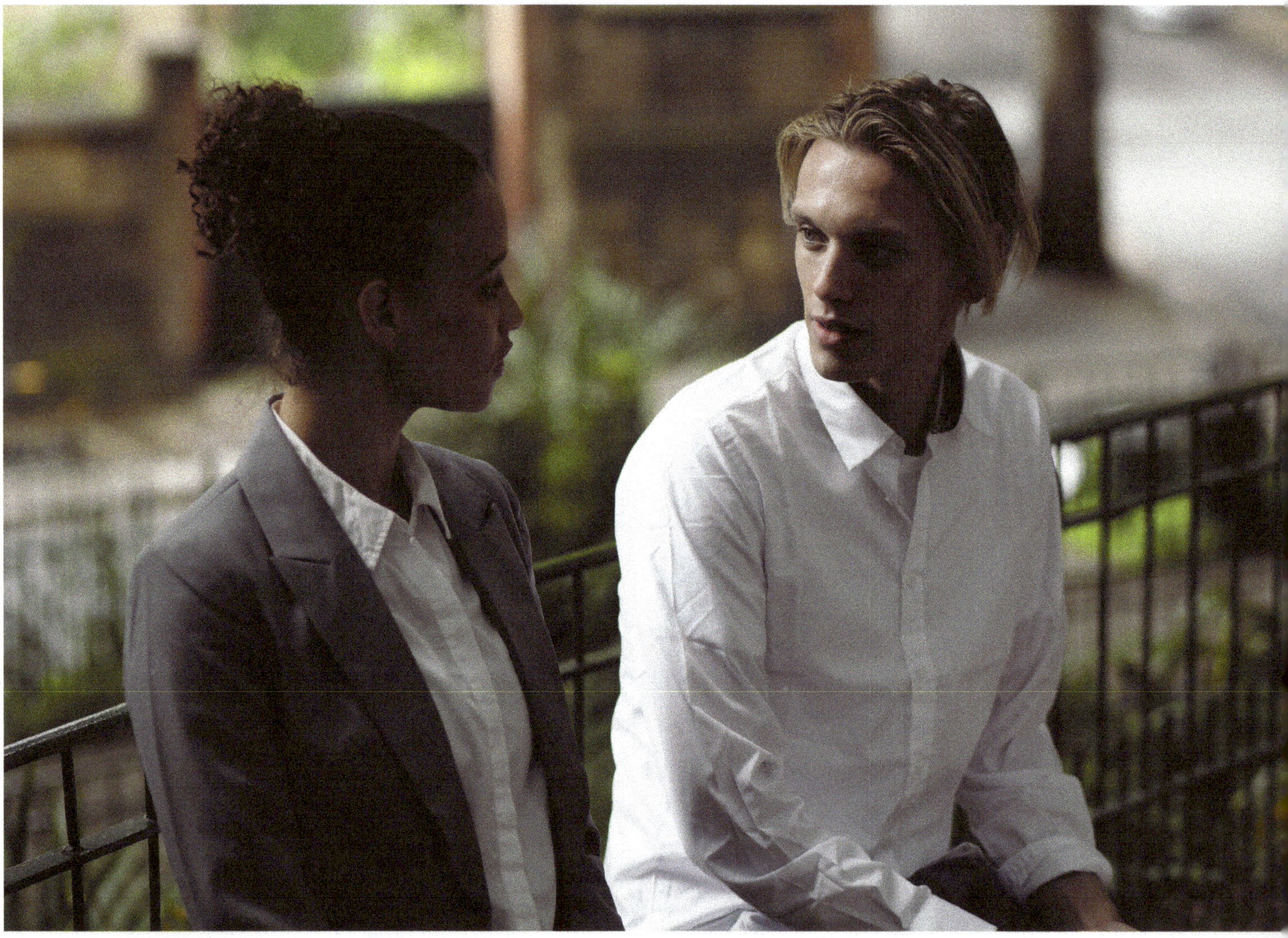

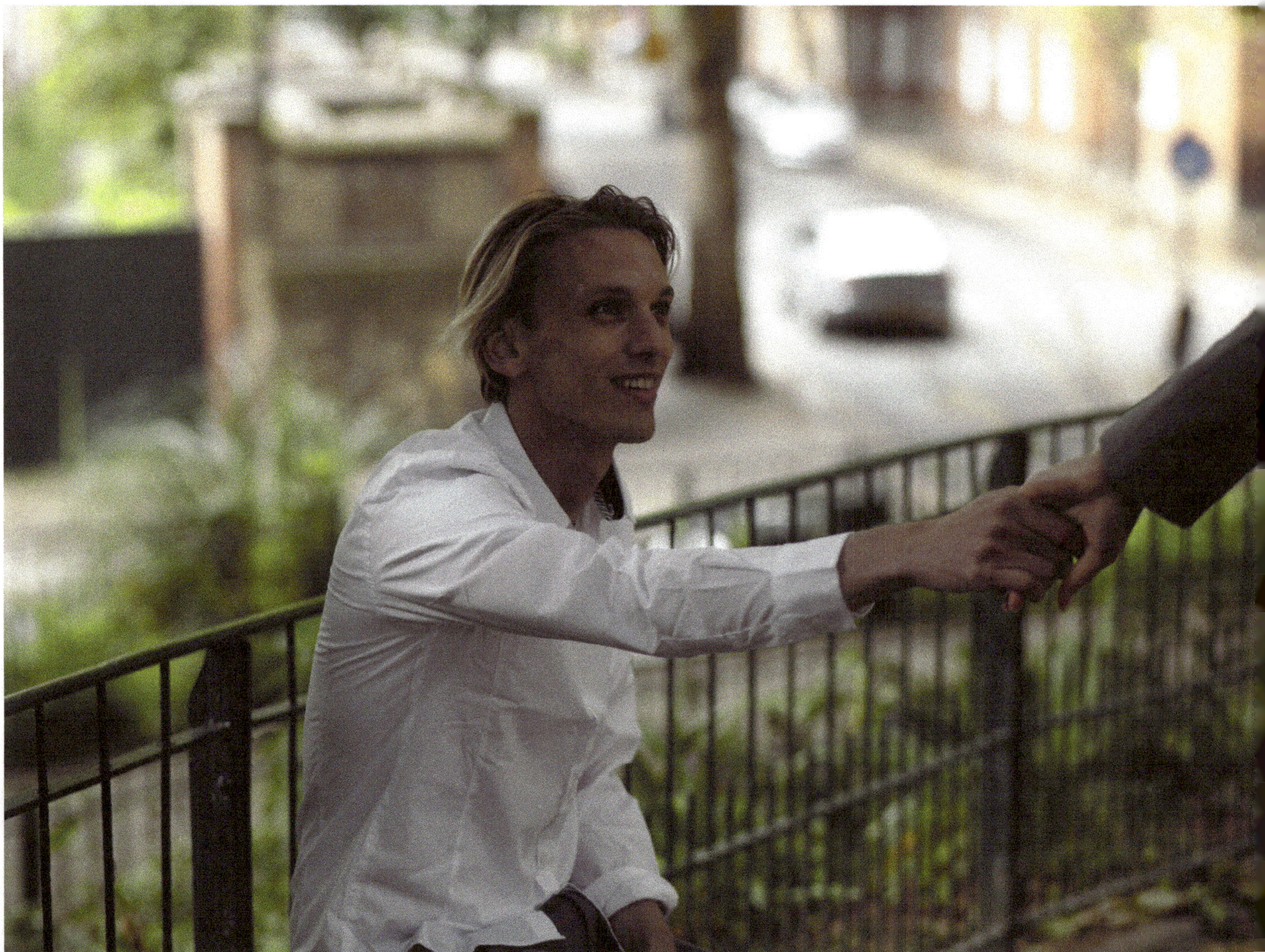

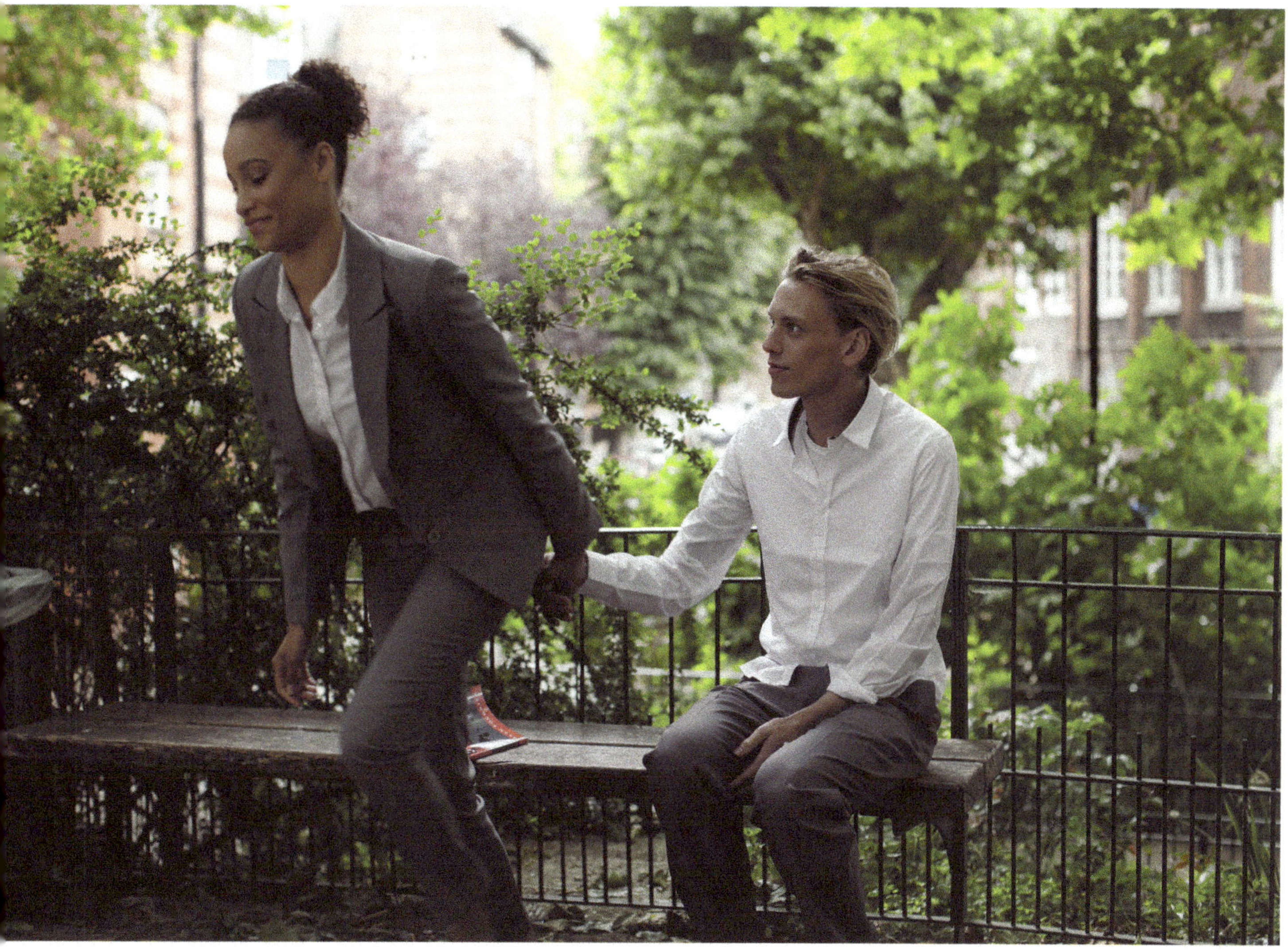

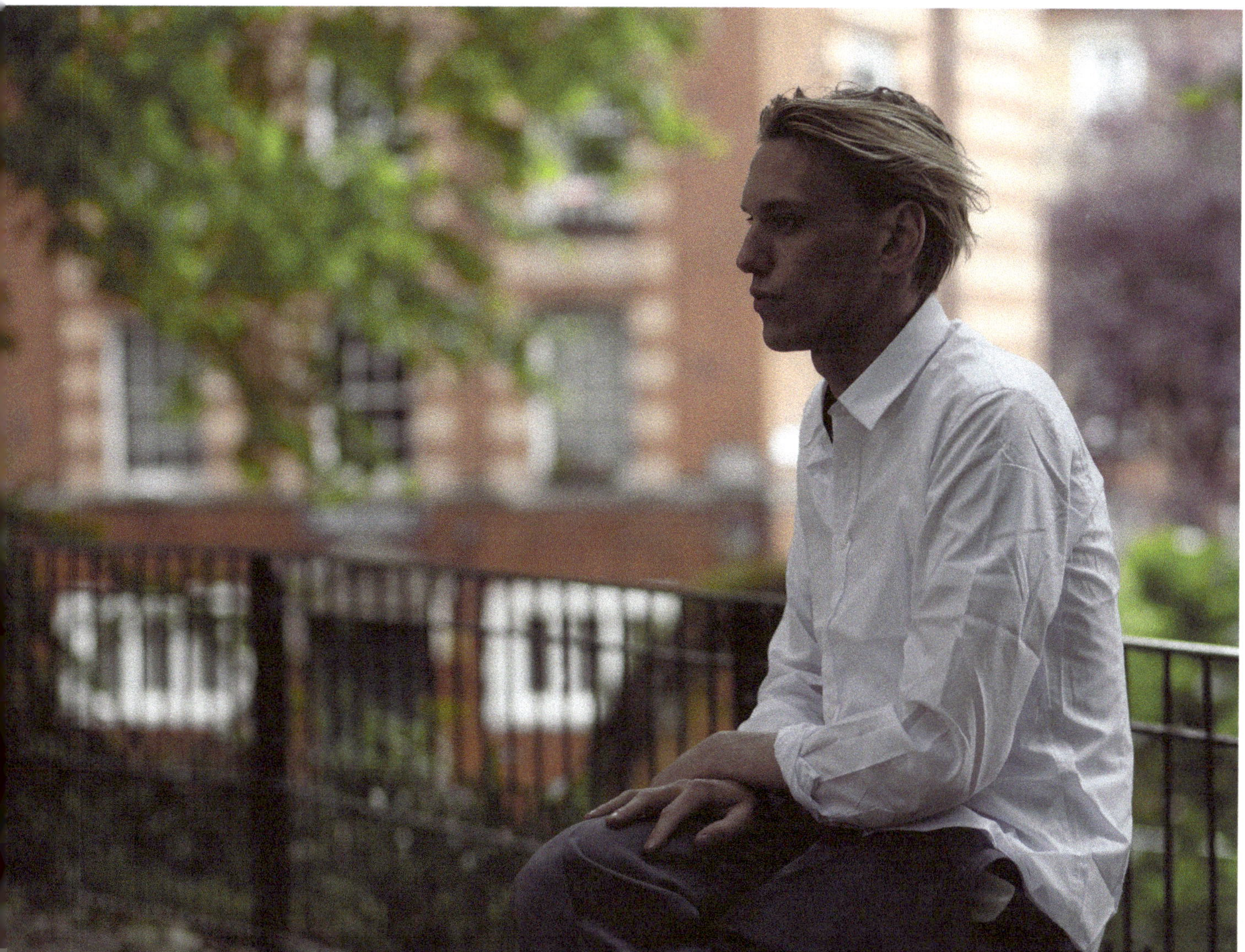

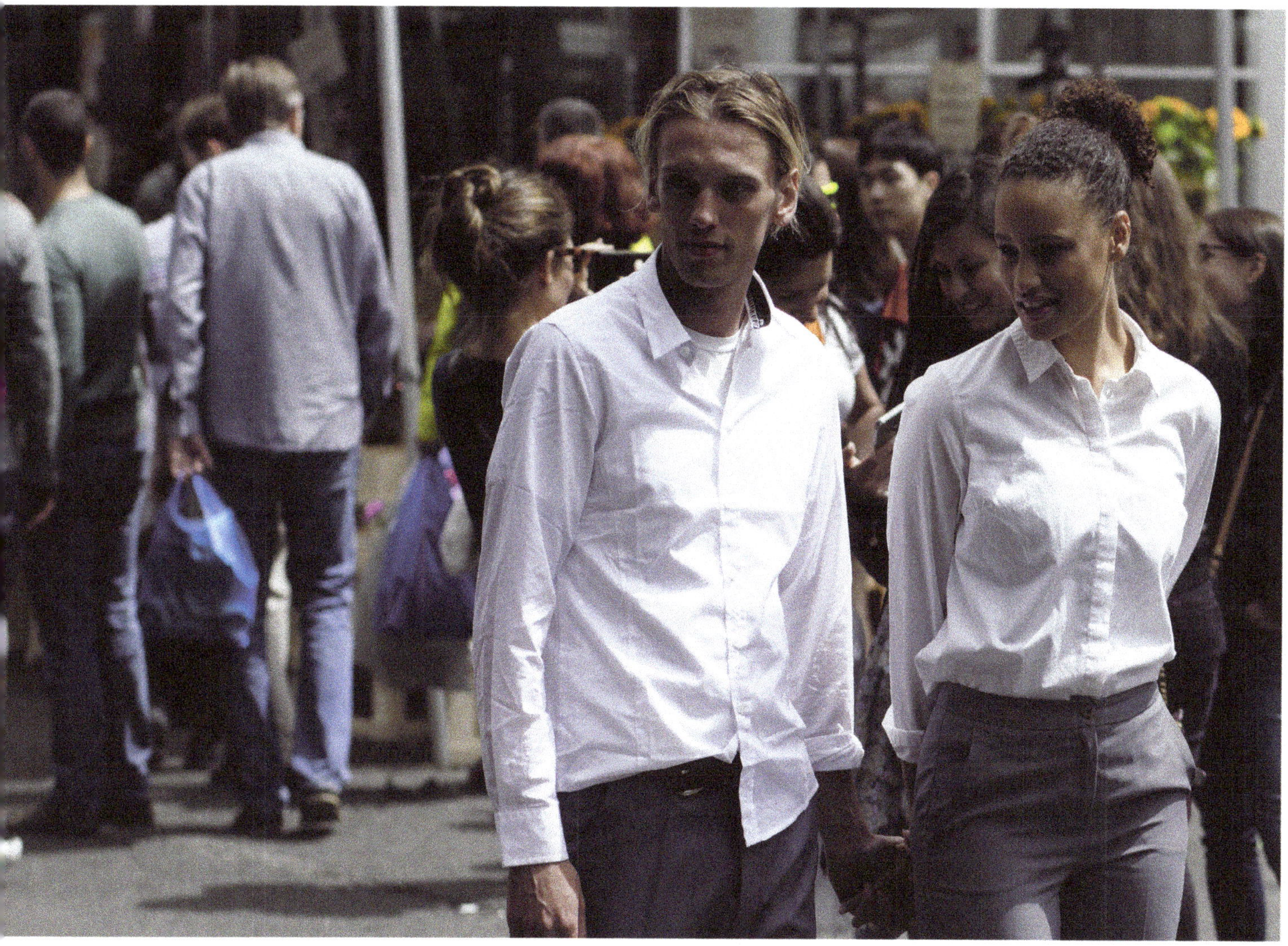

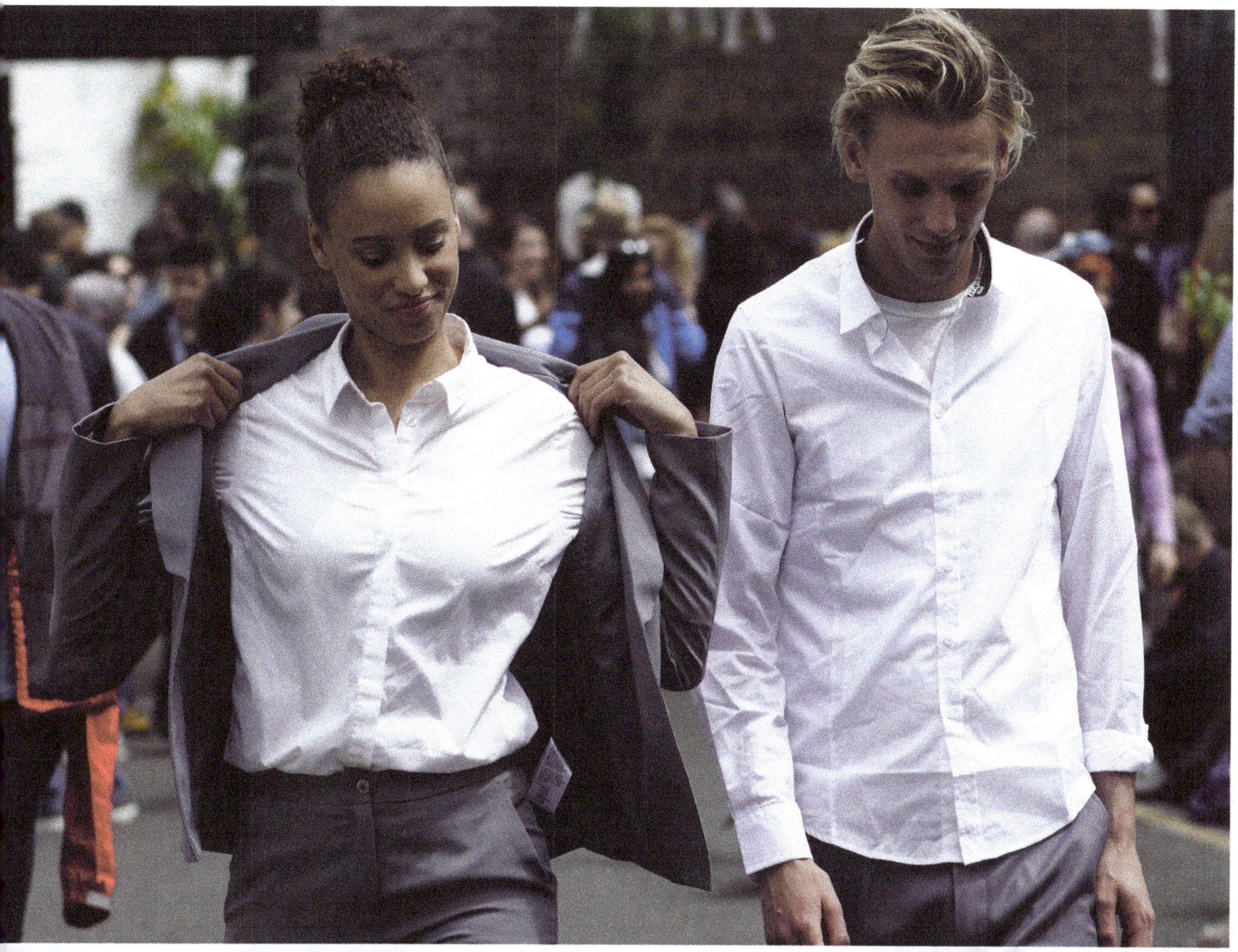

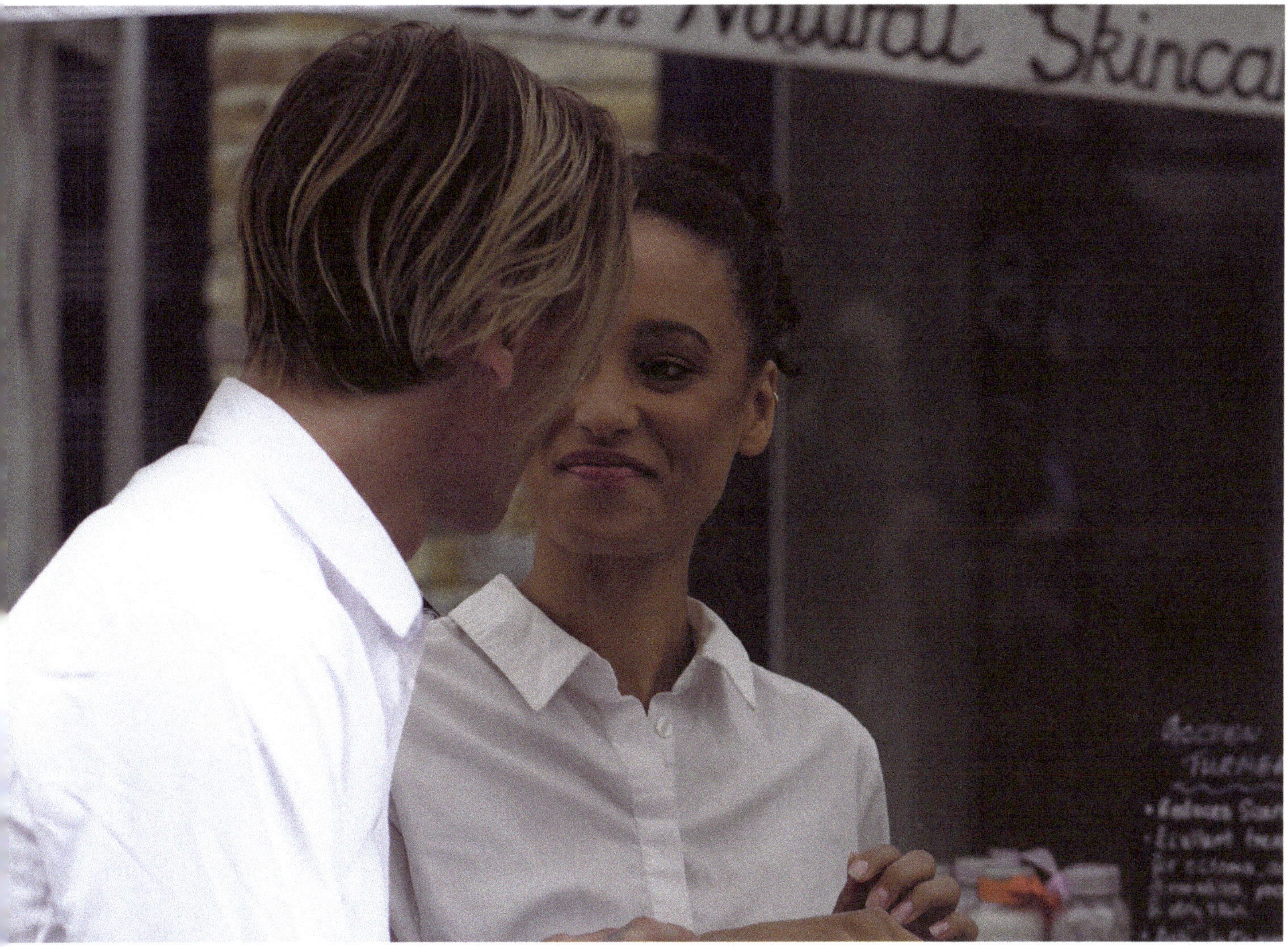
Natural

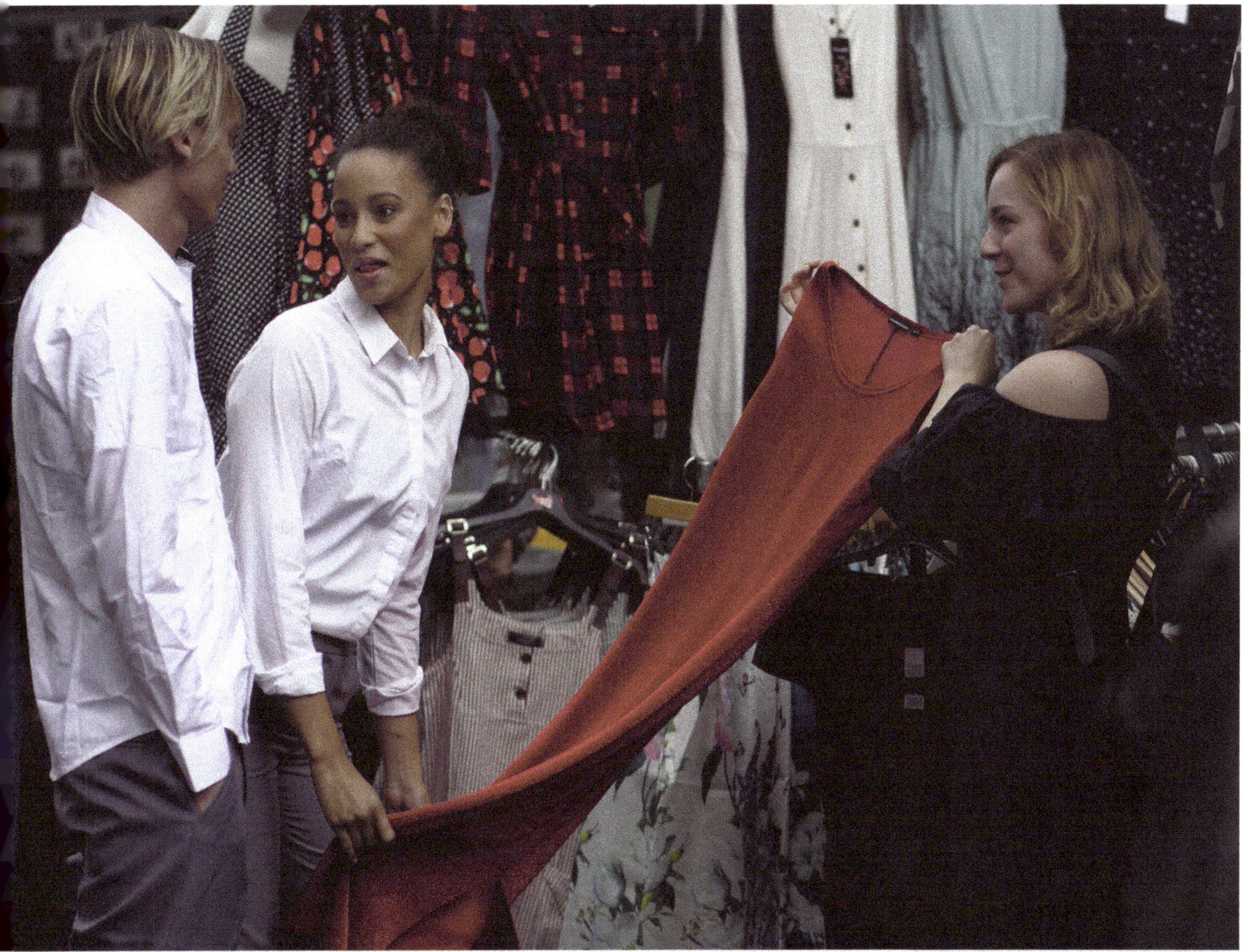

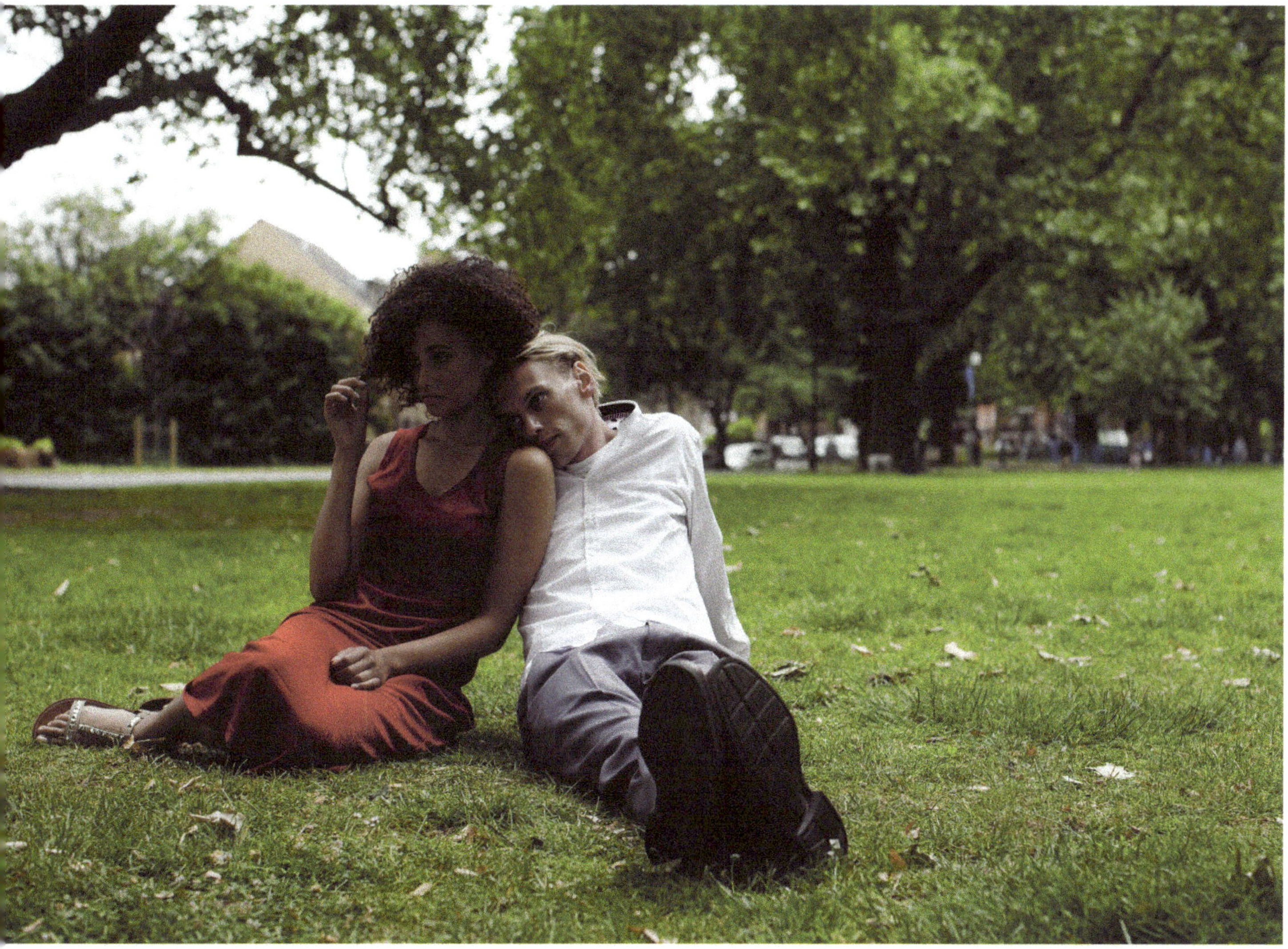

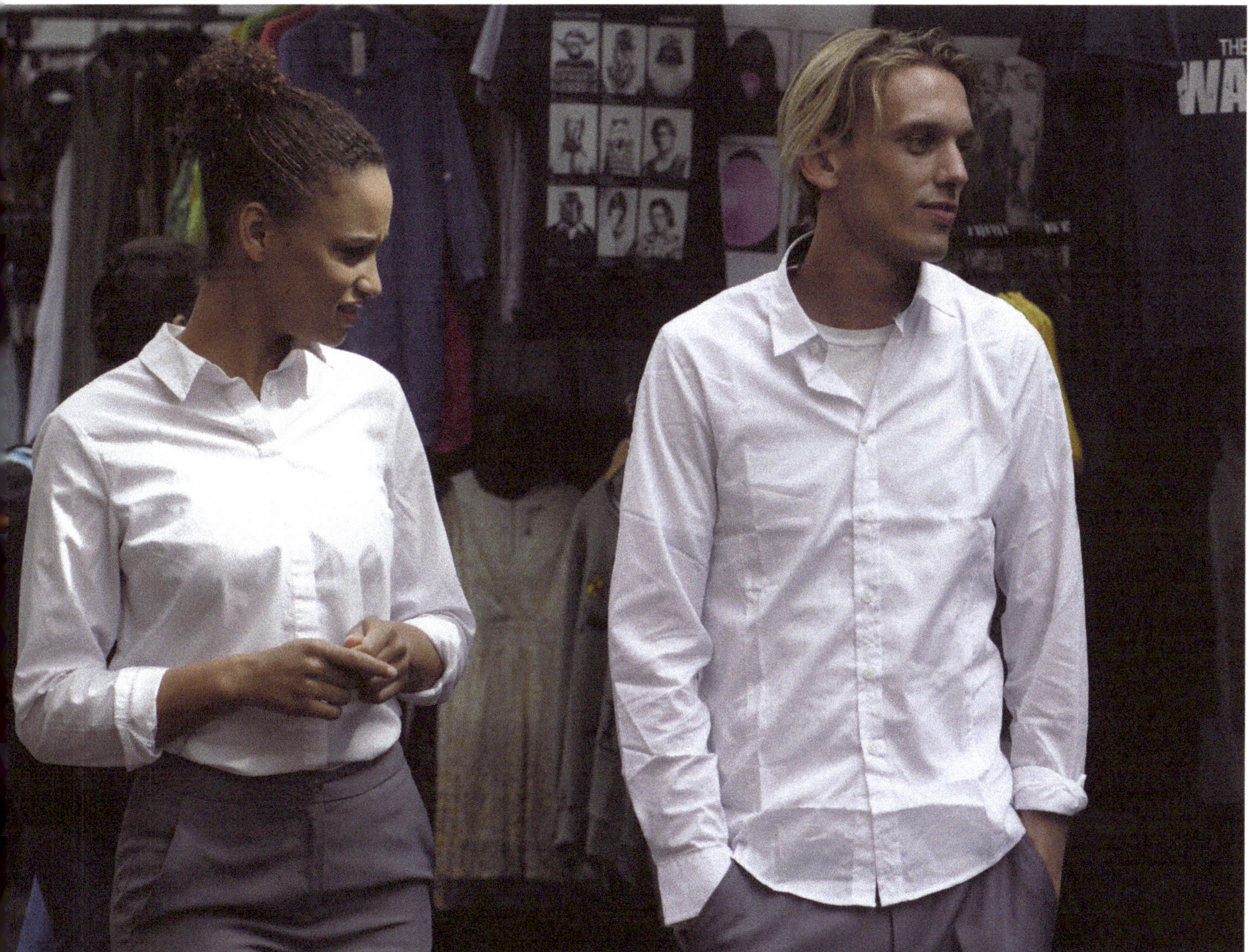

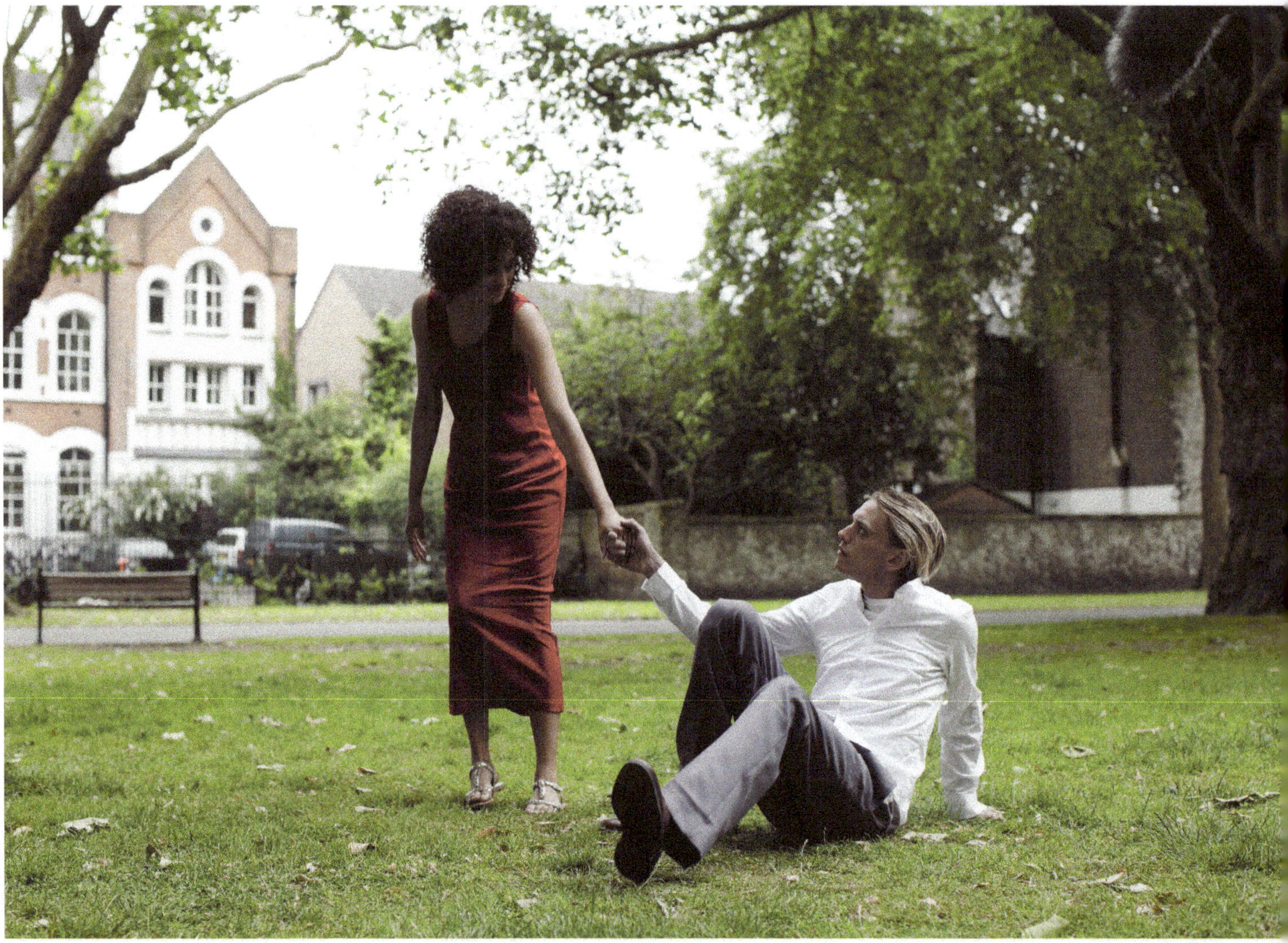

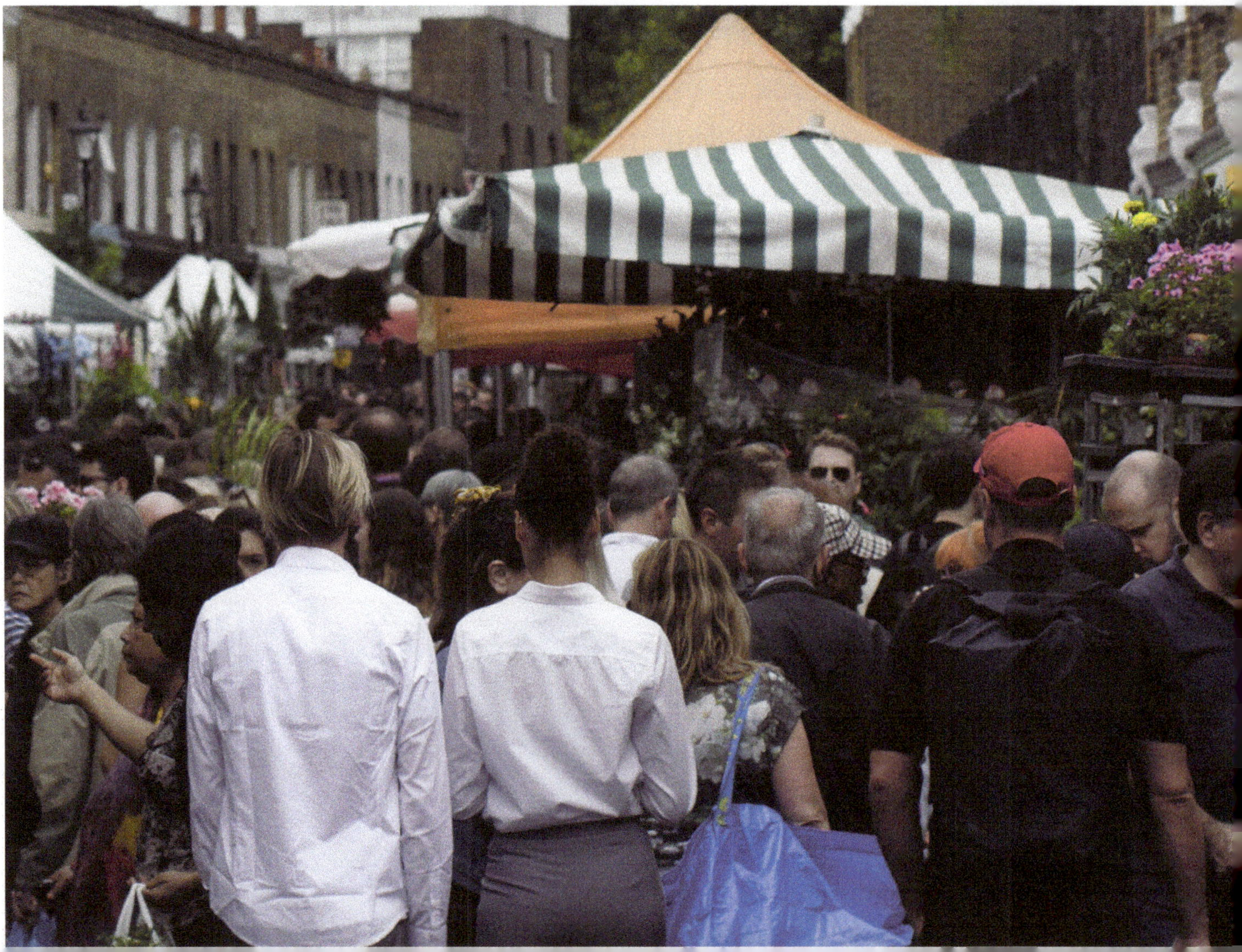

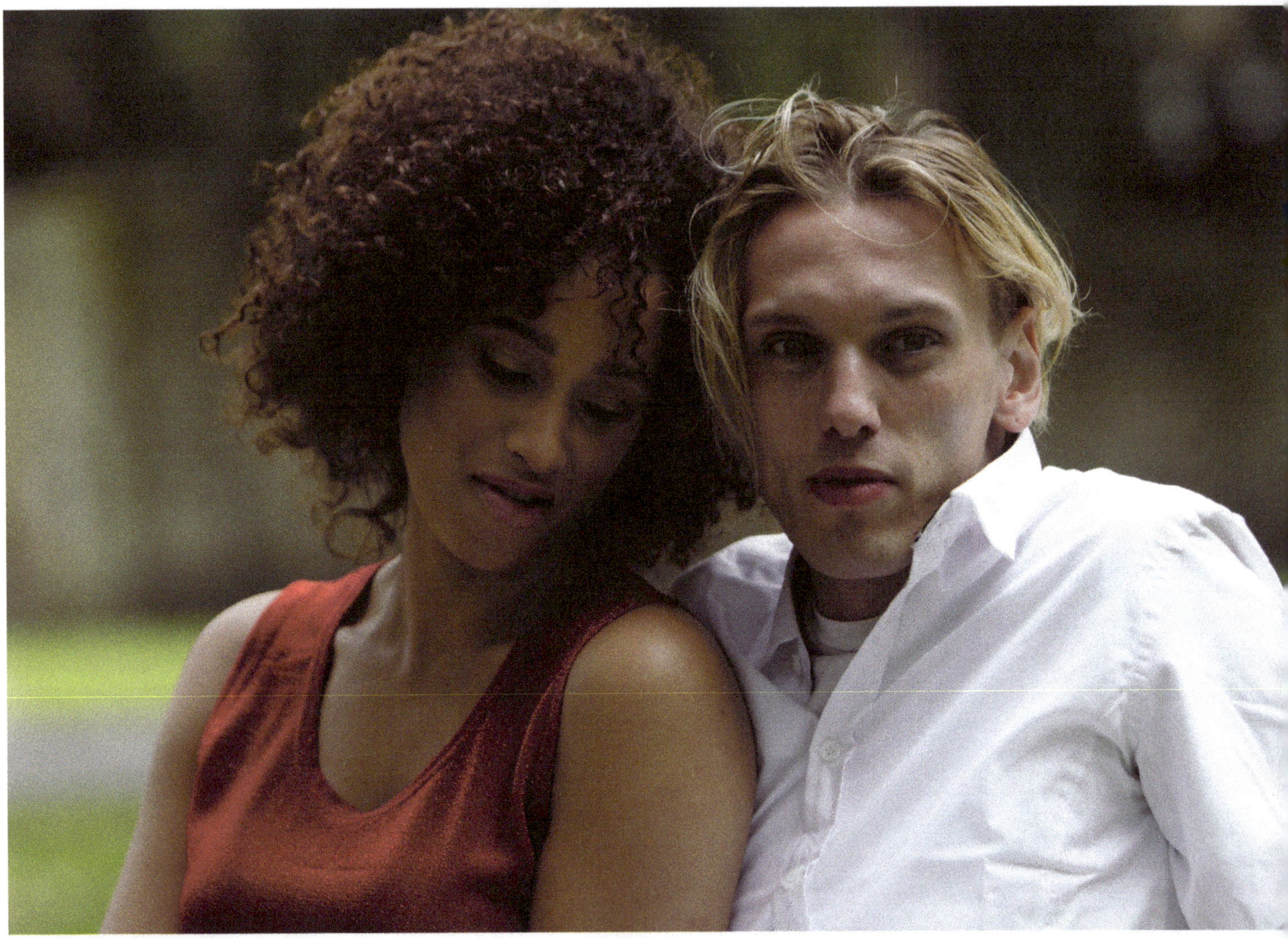

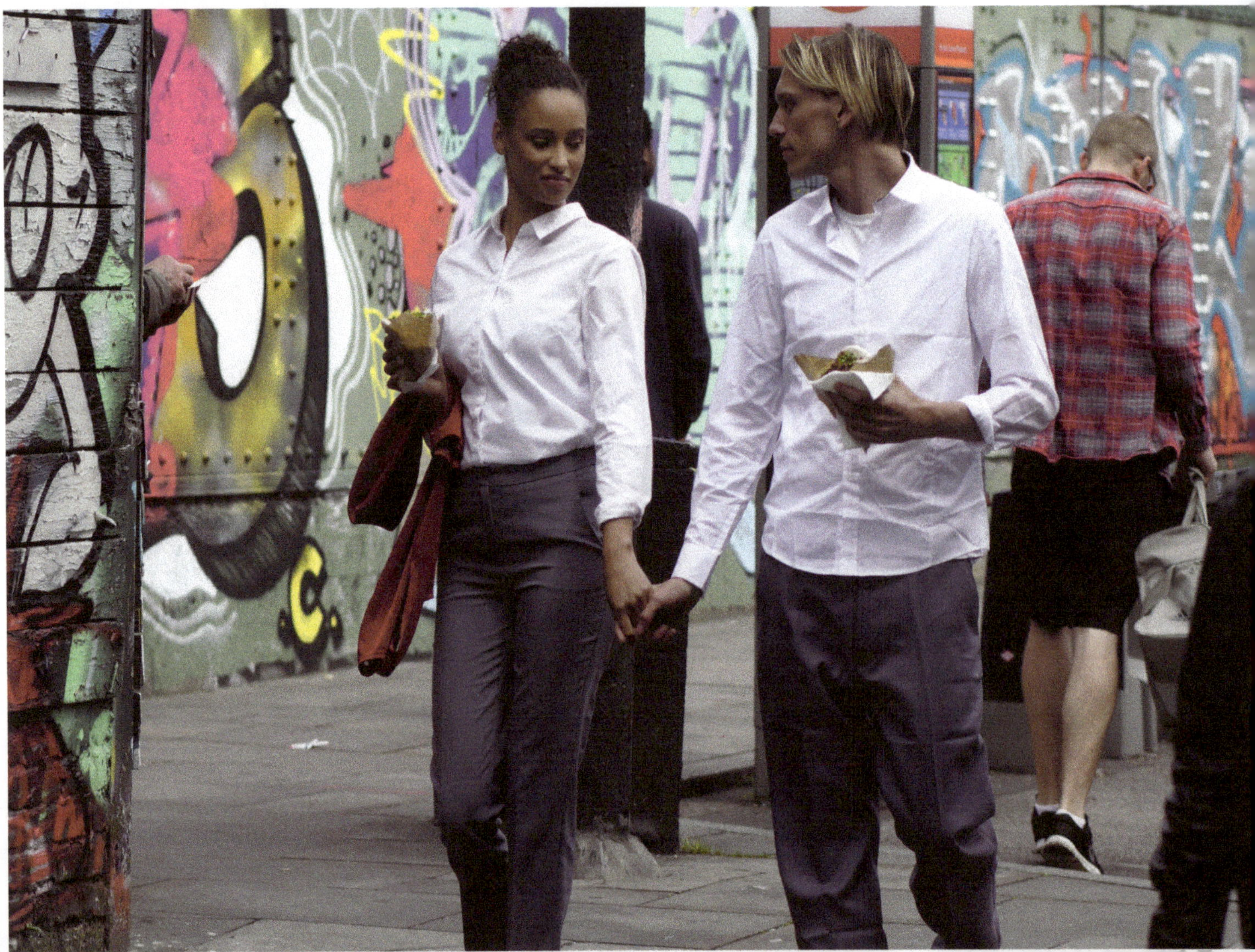

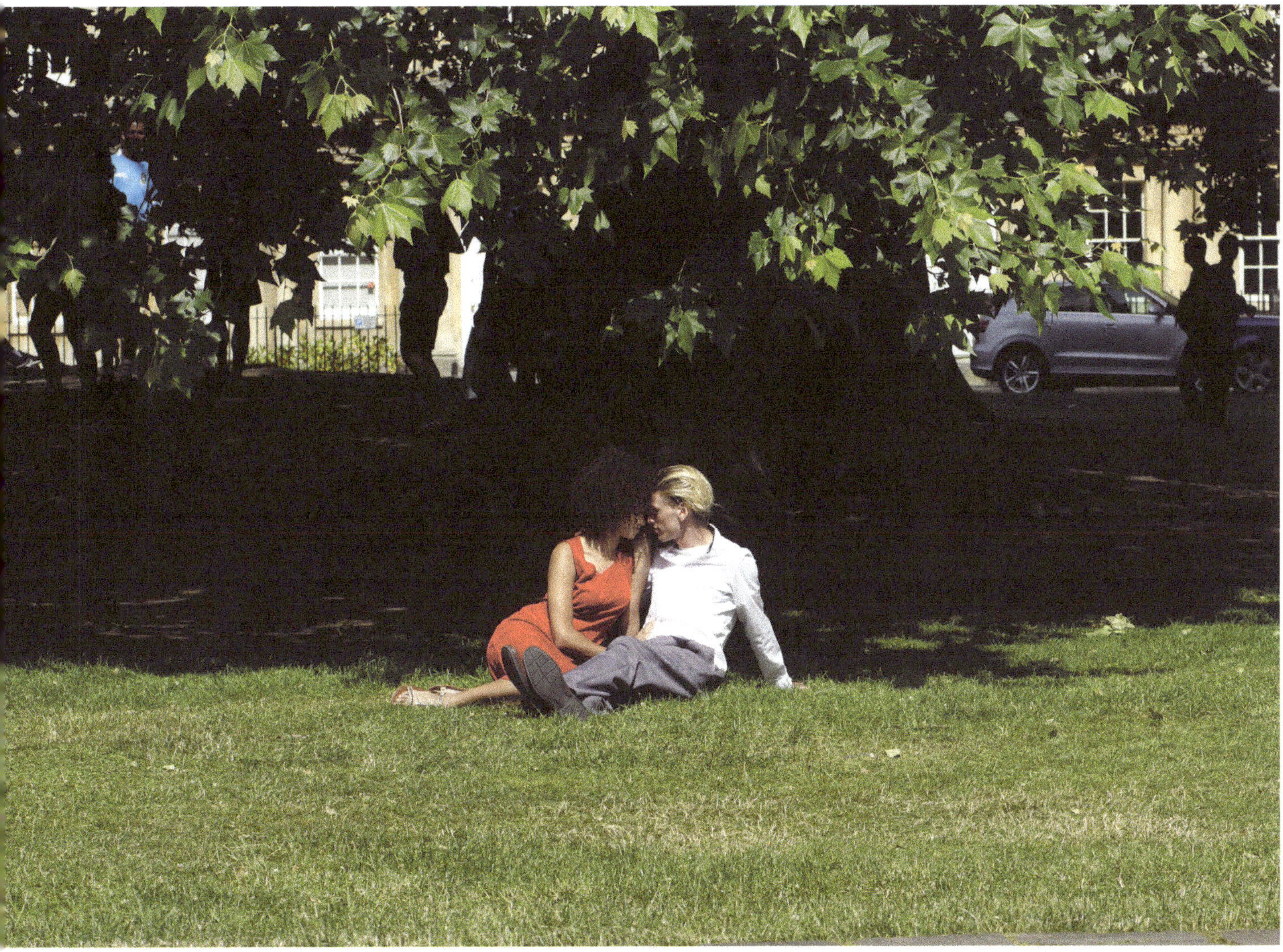

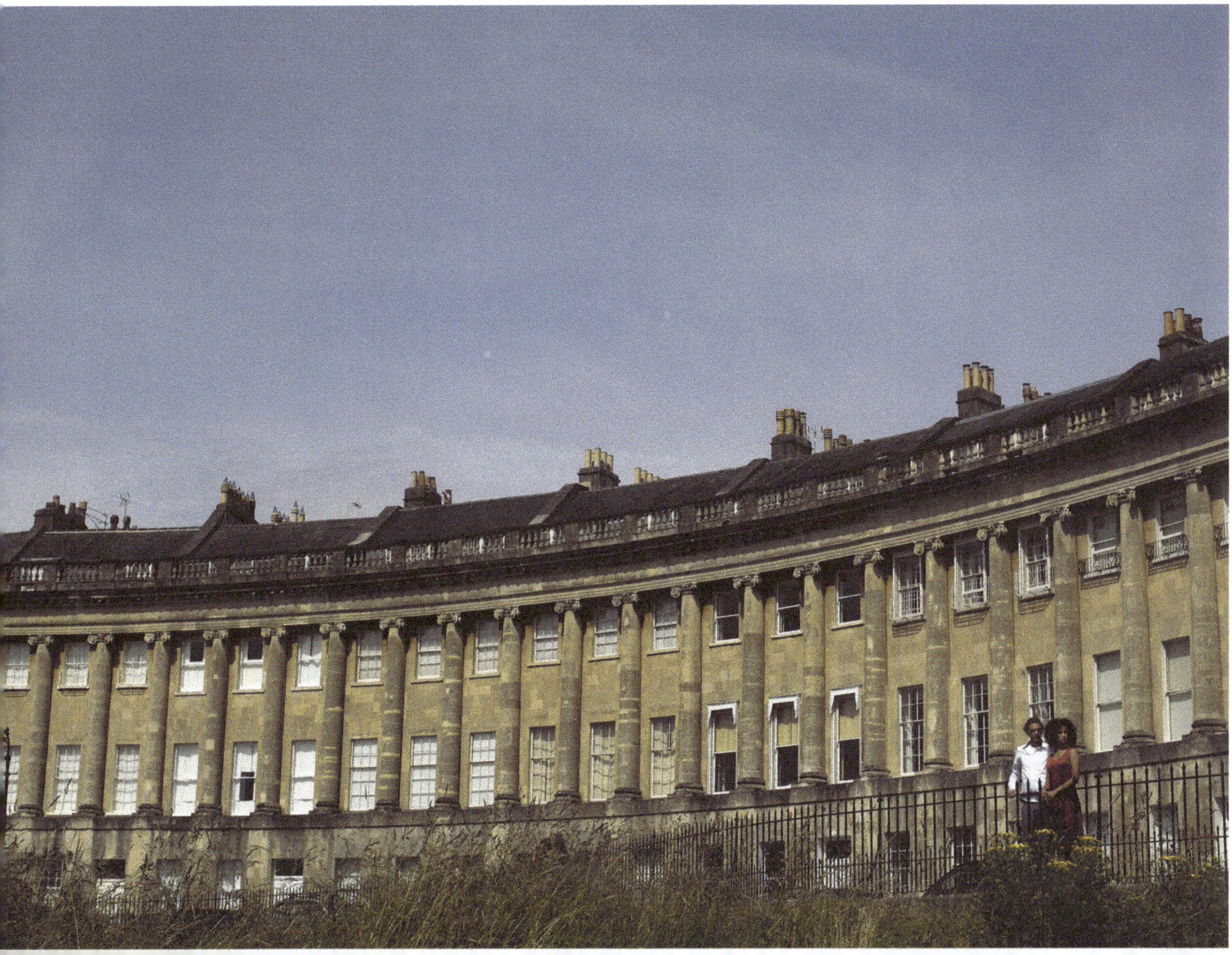

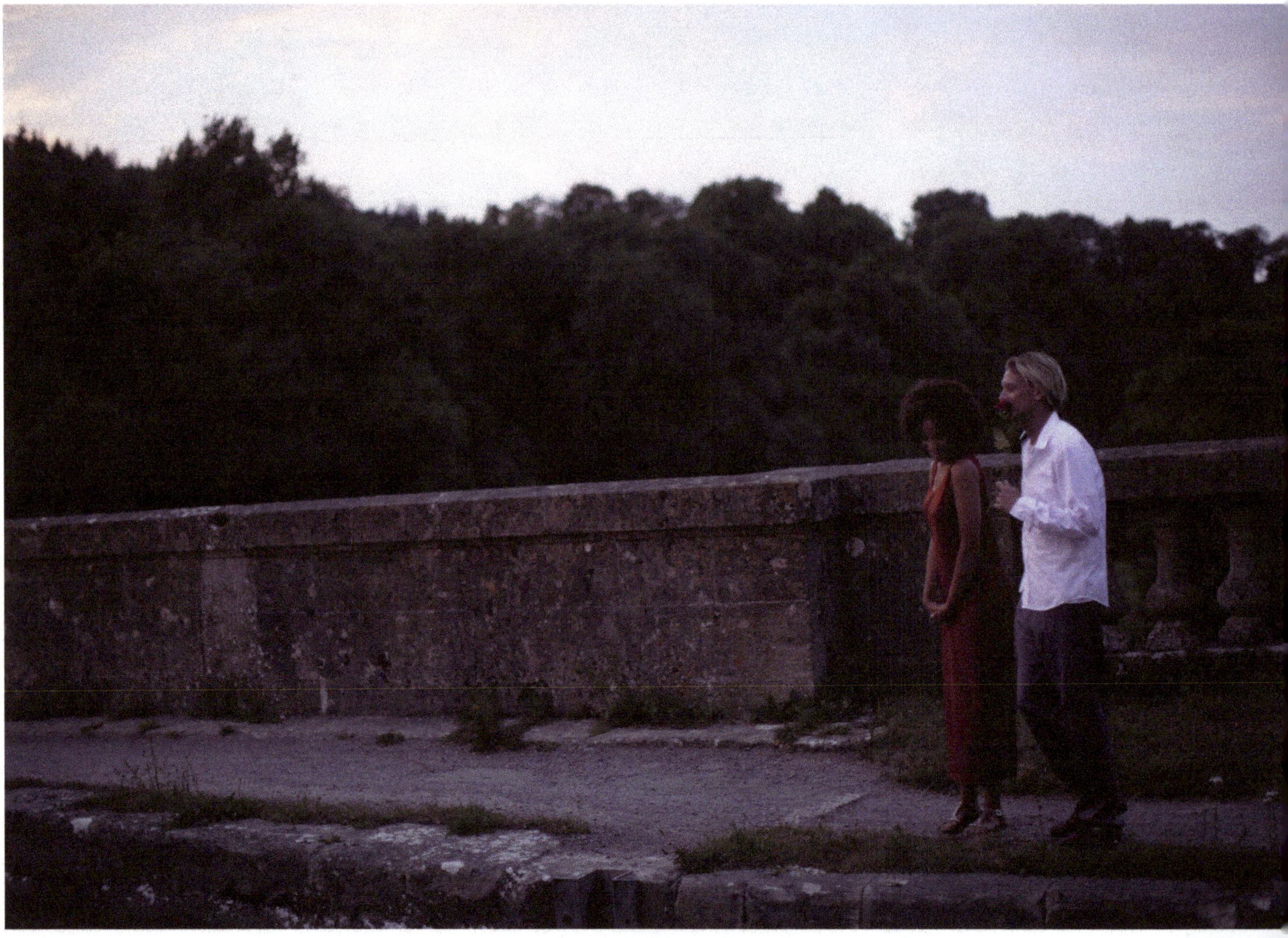

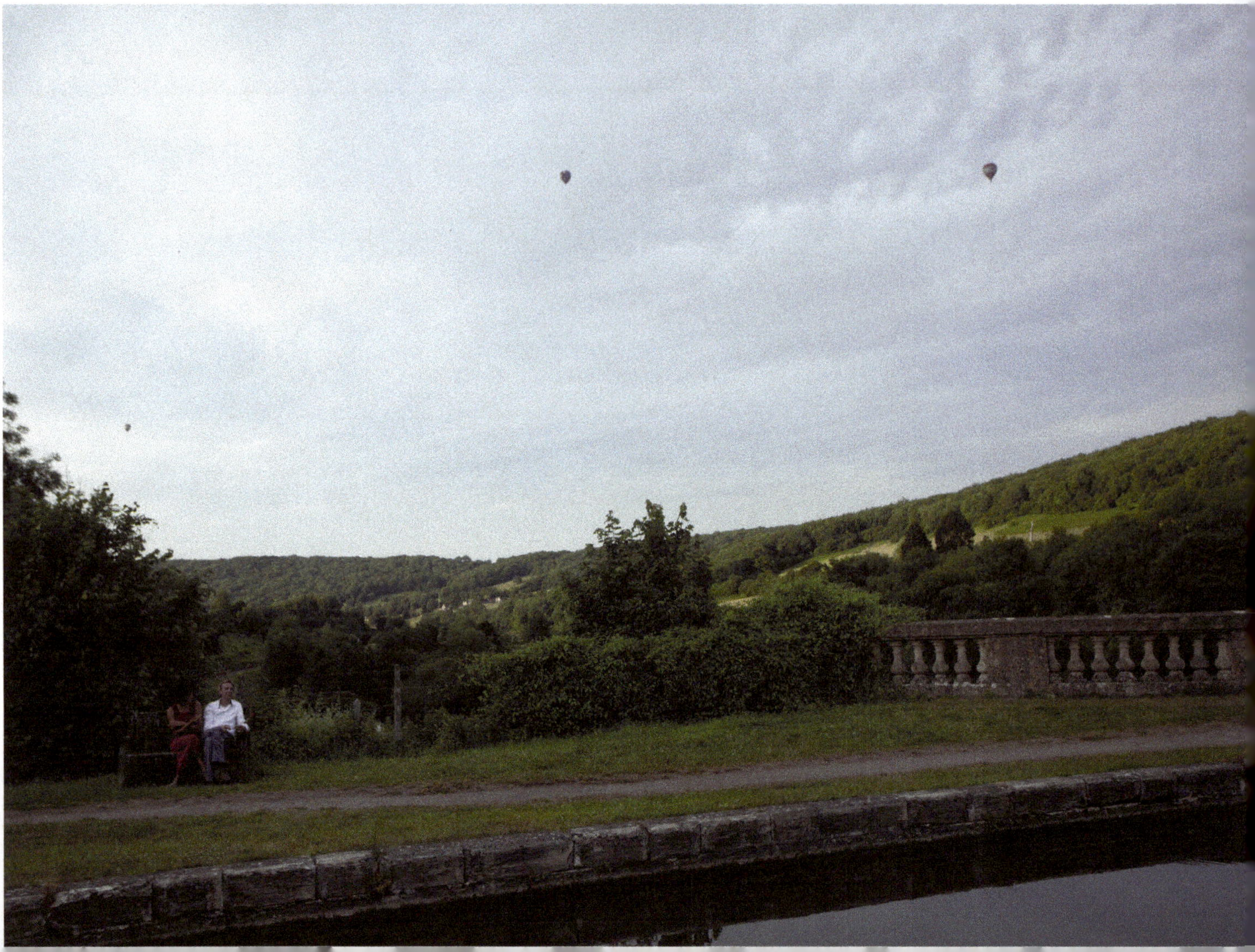

LOCATIONS

- LOCATIONS -

- LONDON -

WEST INDIA QUAYS - JEAN-BAPTISTE'S OFFICE
HERTSMERE RD, CANARY WHARF, LONDON E14 4AE

TOWER HAMLETS - SISTINE'S OPENING
REDCHURCH STREET, LONDON, E2 7DD

HACKNEY - FIELD OF CONTEMPLATION
LONDON FIELDS, HACKNEY, LONDON, E8 3EU

HAMMERWOOD PARK - SISTINE'S HOME, ABSTRACT SEQUENCES
HAMMERWOOD, EAST GRINSTEAD RH19 3QE

COLUMBIA ROAD FLOWER MARKET
COLUMBIA RD, LONDON E2 7RG

BRICK LANE
BRICK LANE, SHOREDITCH, E1 6QL

ARNOLD CIRCUS - JEAN BAPTISTE AND SISTINE ENCOUNTER
ARNOLD CIRCUS, LONDON, E2 7JS

BUCKS BARBERS - JEAN BAPTISTE'S RETURN
83 KINGSLAND ROAD, LONDON, E2 8AG

- BATH -

THE ROYAL CRESENT
ROYAL CRESCENT, BATH, BA1 2LR

THE CIRCUS
THE CIRCUS, BATH, BA1 2EW

DUNDAS AQUEDUCT
BRASSKNOCKER BASIN, MONKTON COMBE BA2 7JD

CHARLCOMBE LANE - JEAN BAPTISTE AND SISTINE'S SAFE HAVEN
CHARLCOMBE LANE, LANSDOWN, BATH, BA1 5TT

BEHIND THE SCENES PHOTOS

S.D.O.S
ROLL
#A006
#B004
SCENE
3
SLATE
23
TAKE
1
DIR: RICHARD PERRY
DOP: ROBIN VIDGEON BSC
DATE: 17/06/18
EXT
DAY
SYNC

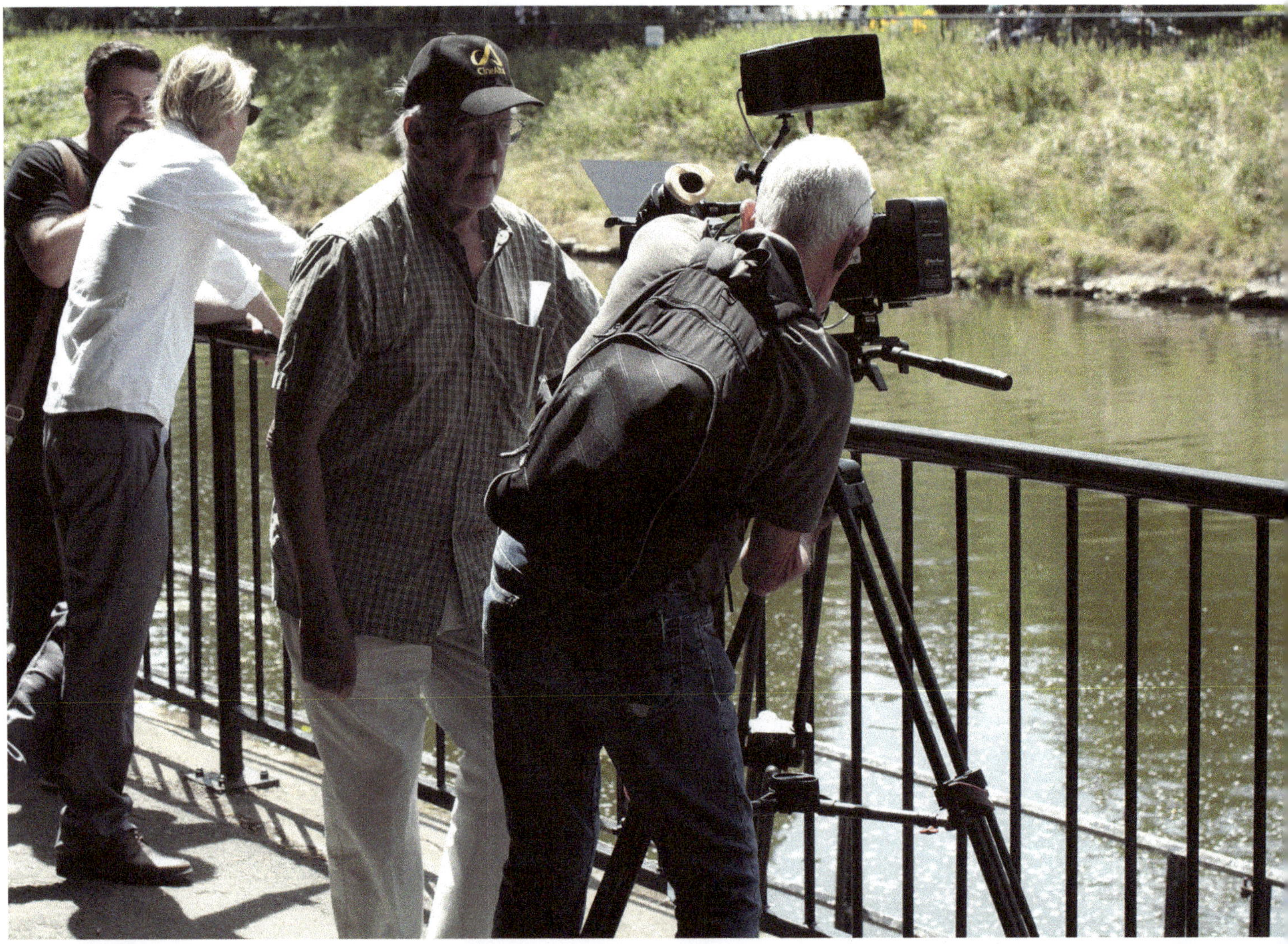

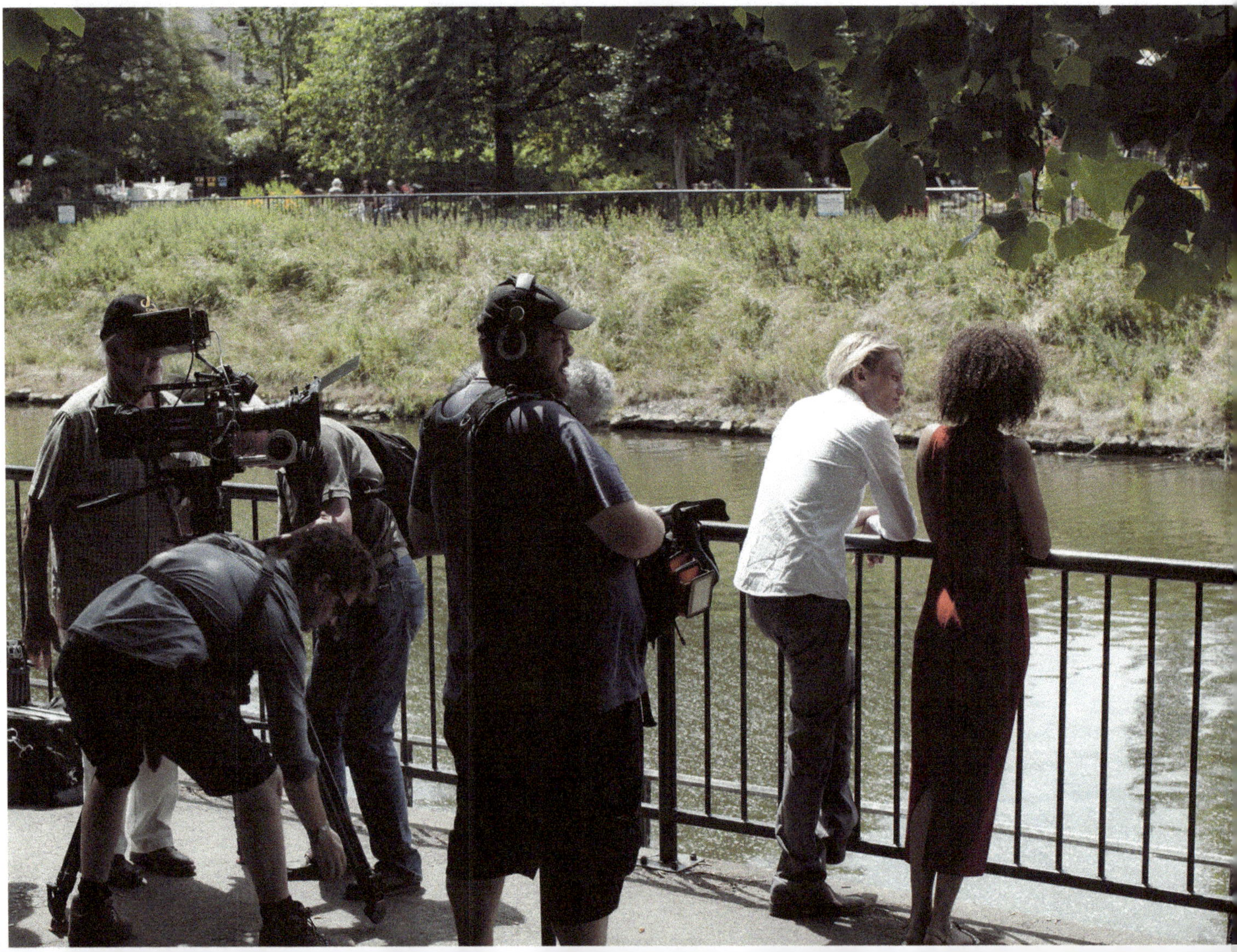

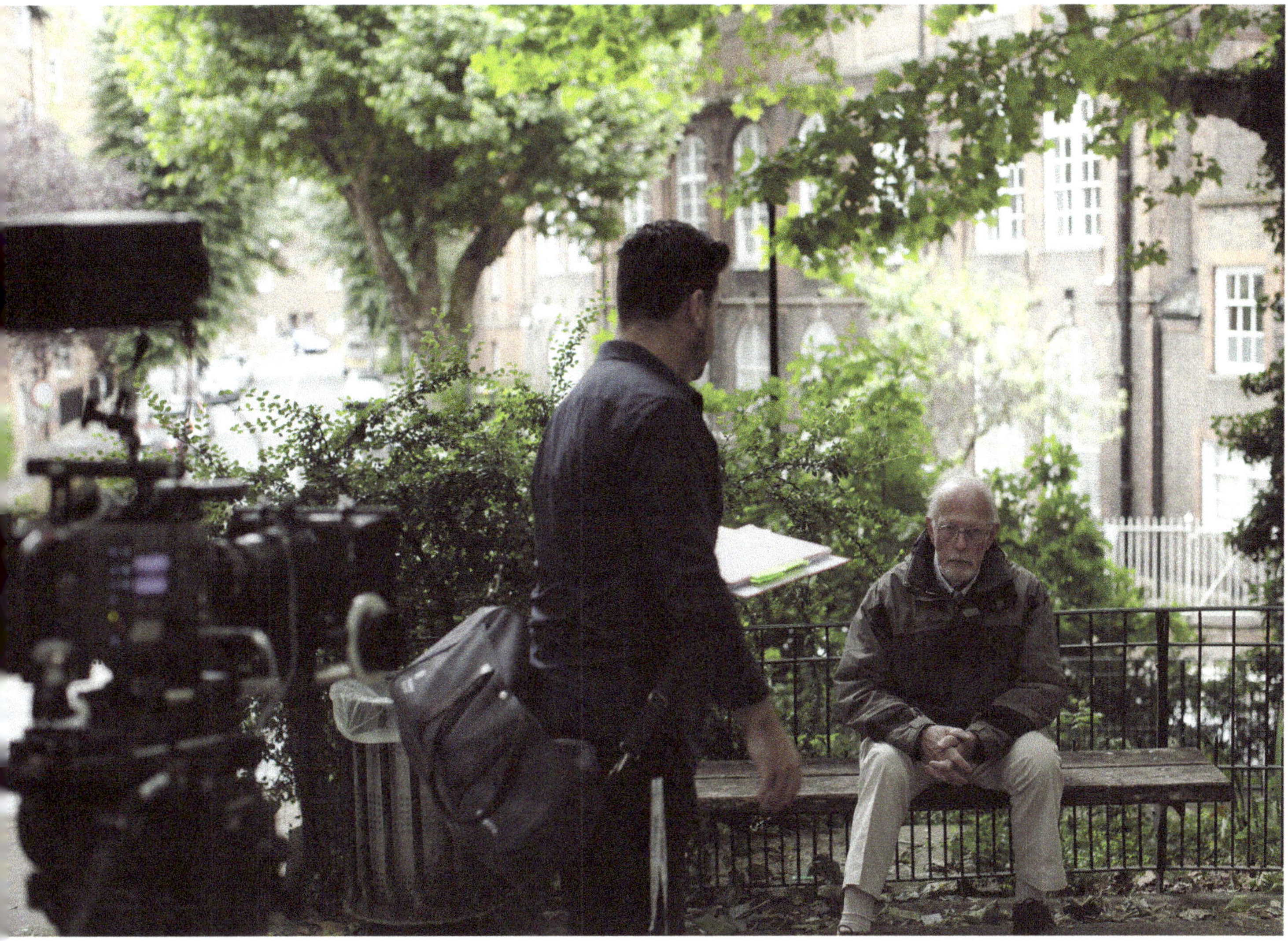

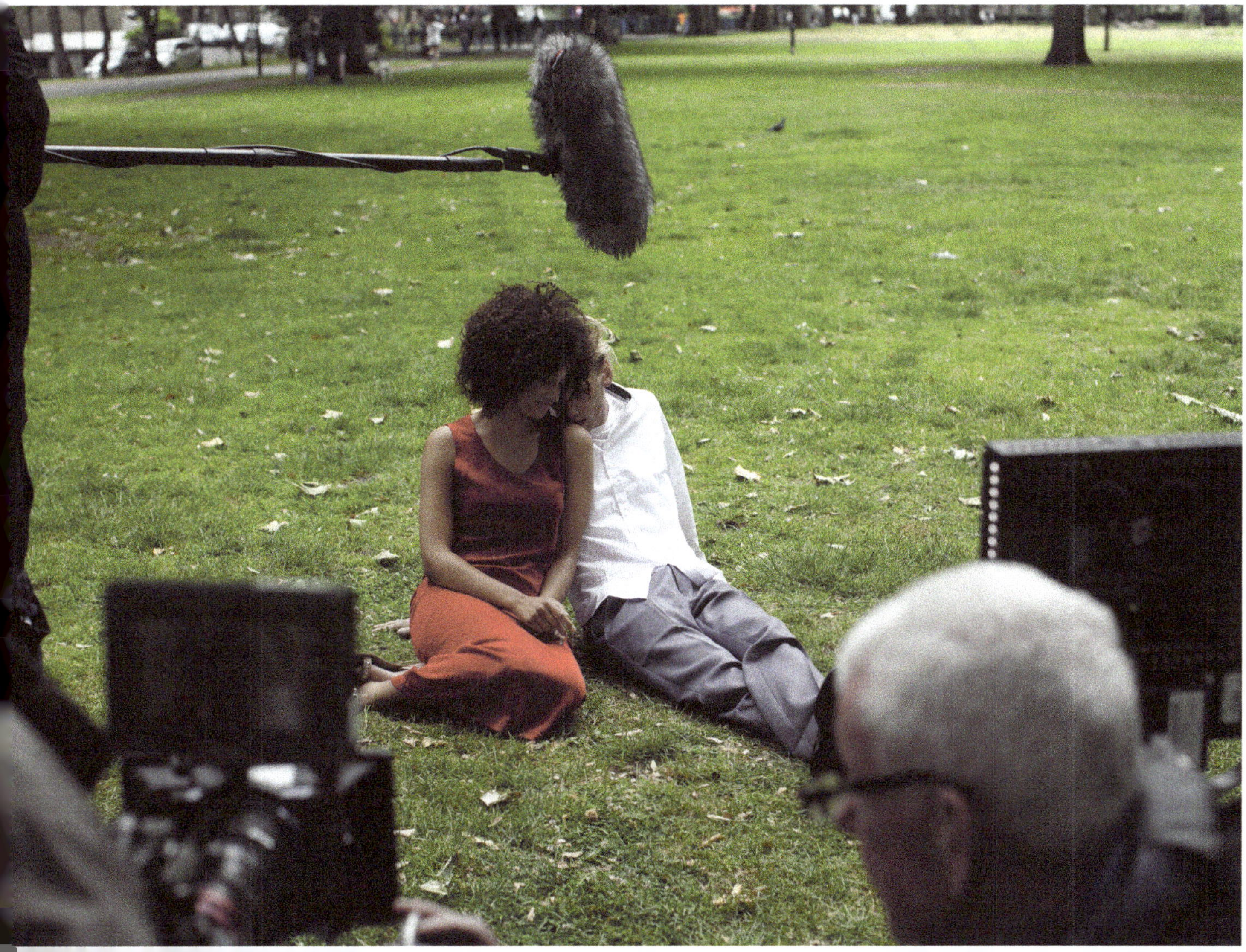

S.D.O.S
ROLL
SLATE
TAKE
#A009
#B007
SCENE
26
2
DIR RICHARD PERRY
DOP ROBIN VIDGEON BSC
DATE 17/06/18
EXT
DAY
SYNC.

S.D.O.S
SLATE
TAKE
139
1
RICHARD PERRY
ROBIN VIDGEON BSC

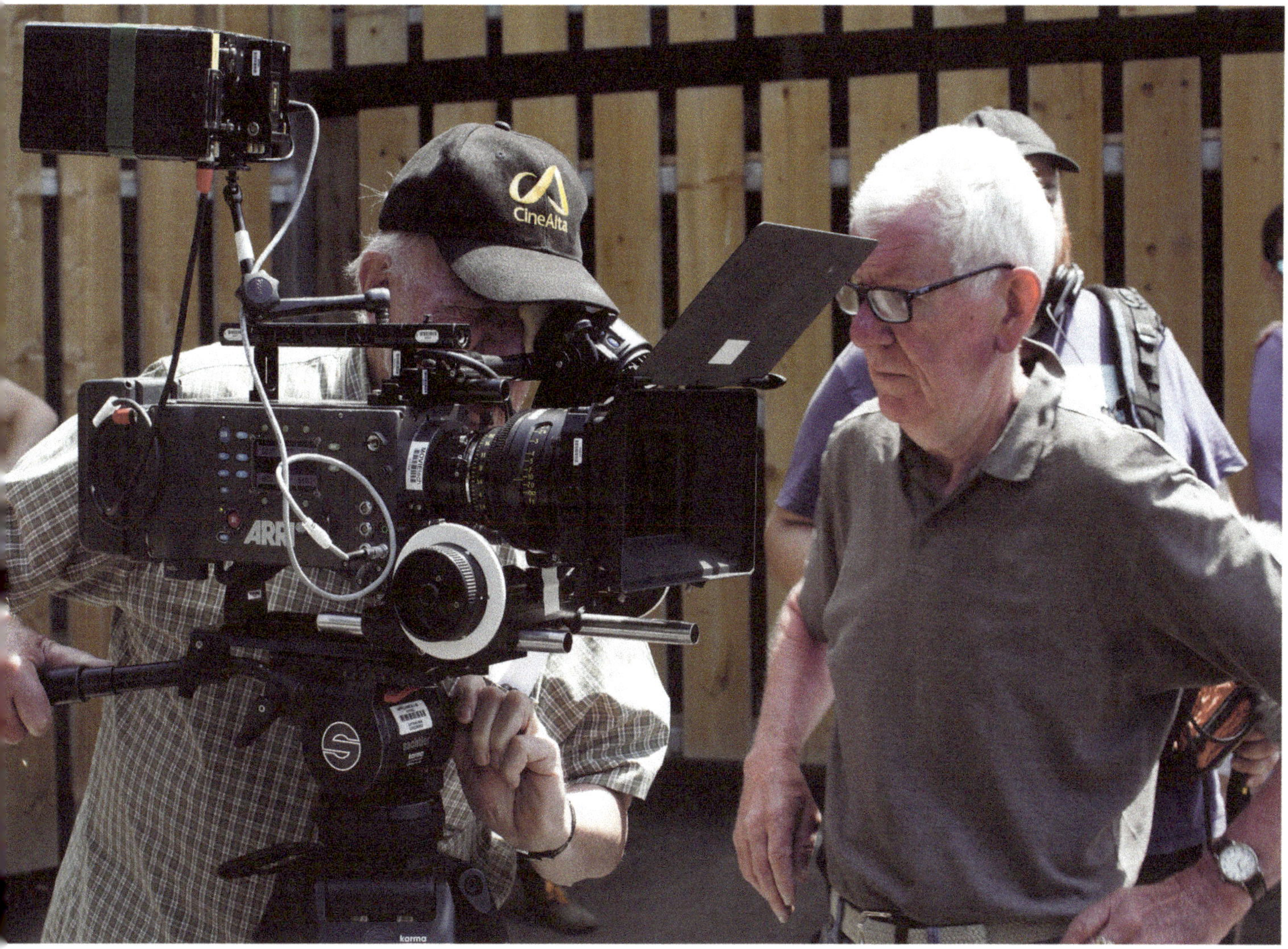
CineAlta
ARRI

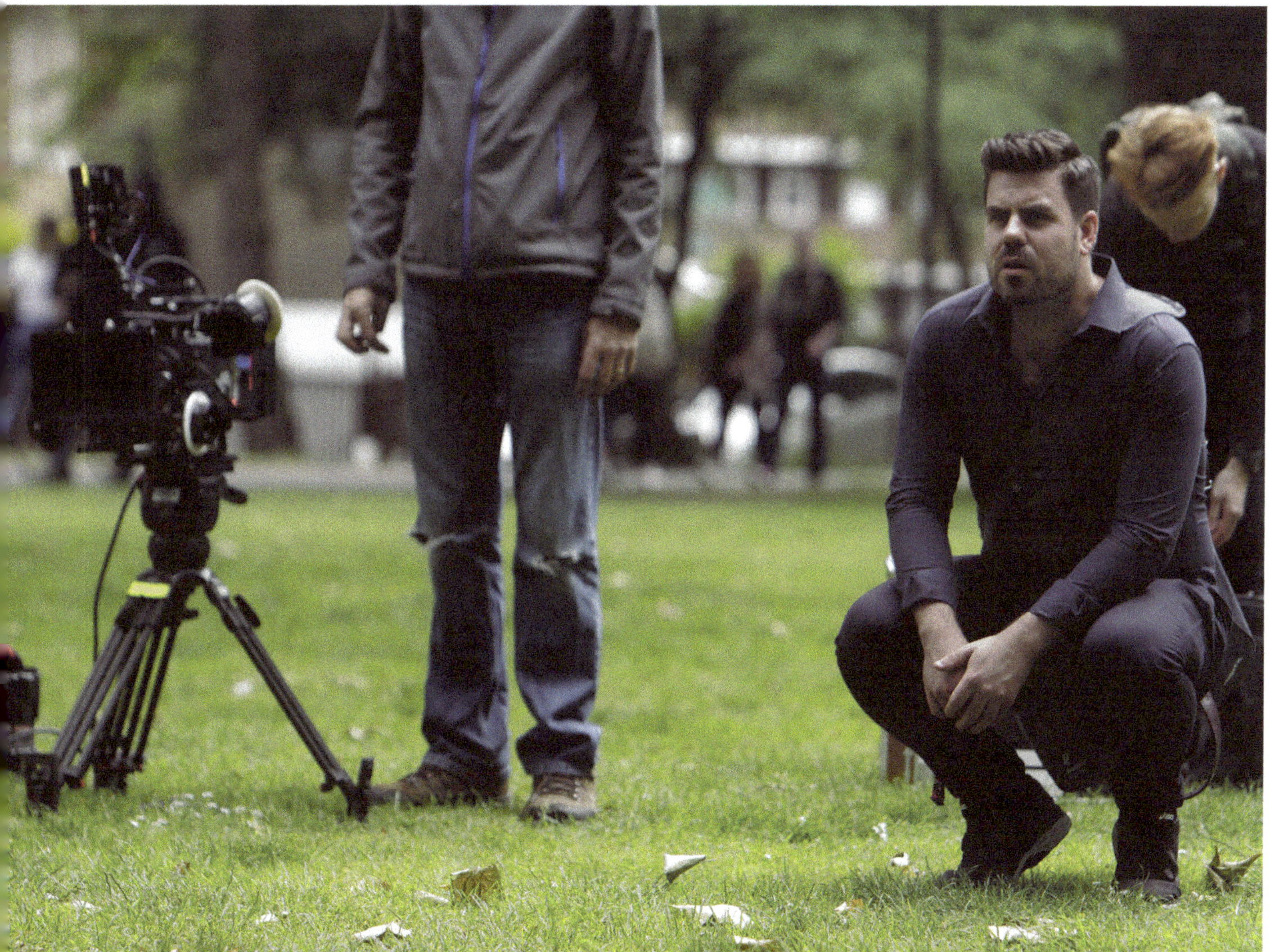

S.D.O.S
26
1
RICHARD PERRY
ROBIN VIDGEON BSC
17/06/18
EXT
DAY
SYNC
ARRI

CineAlta

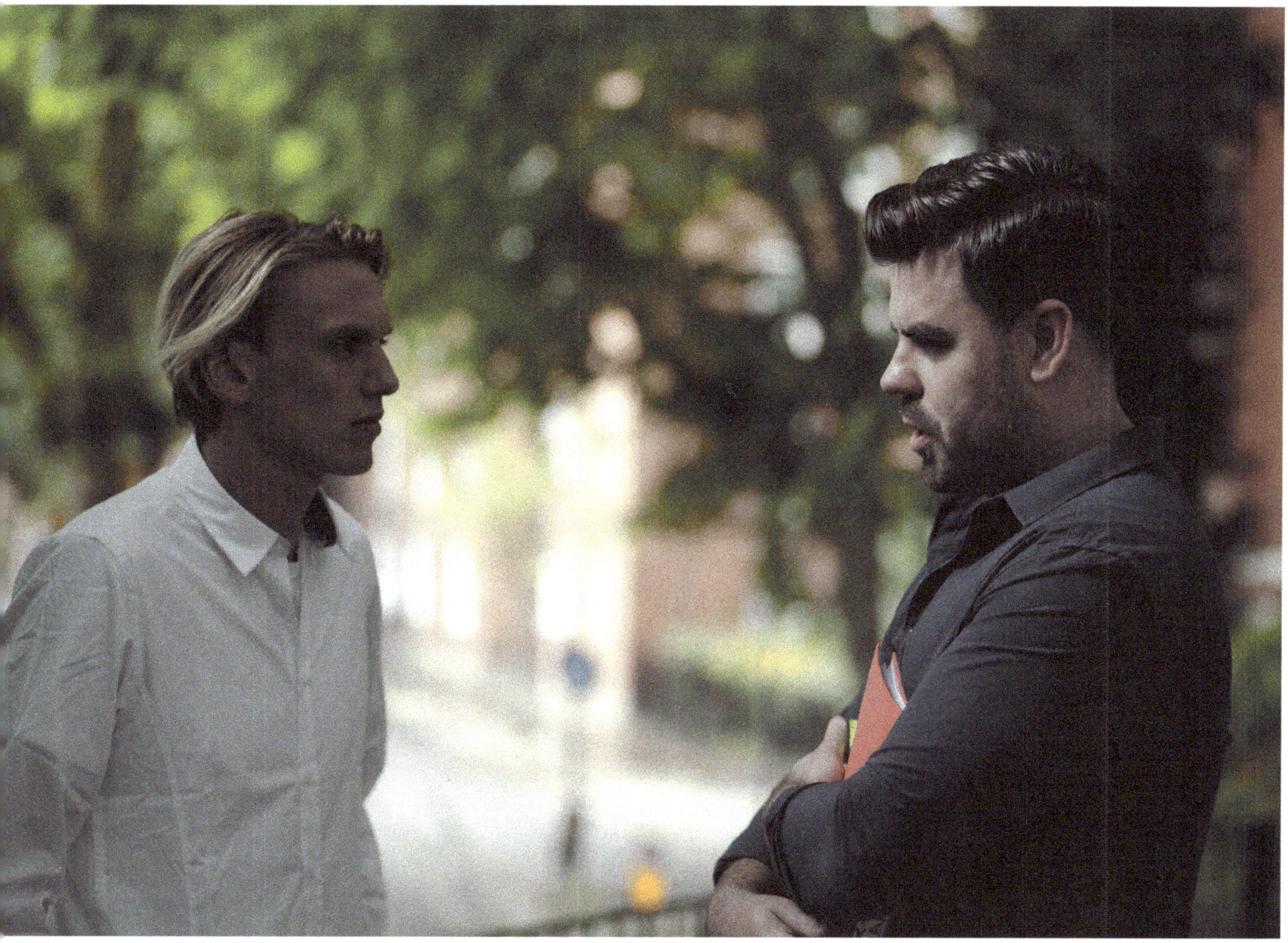

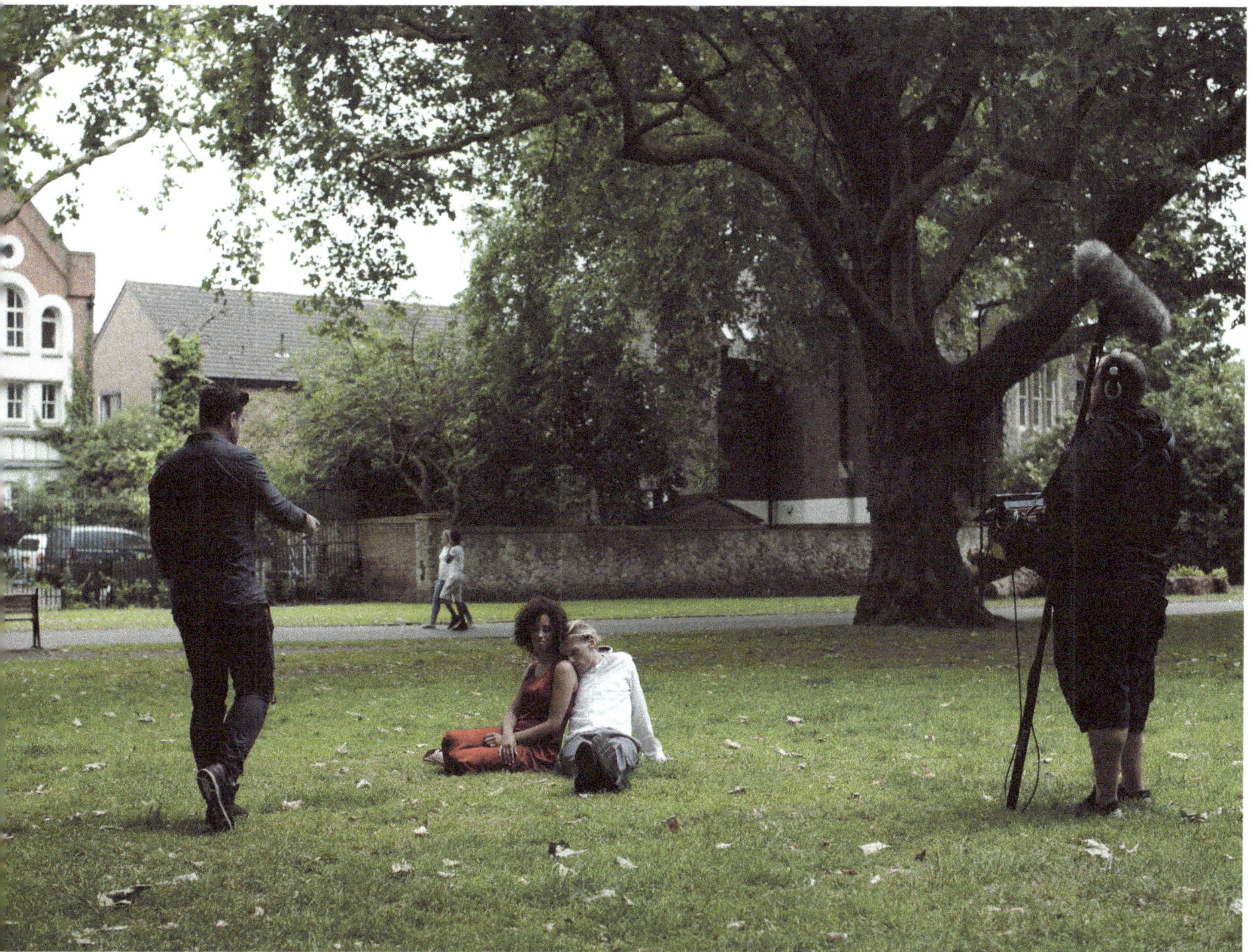

SIX DAYS OF SISTINE

Story and Screenplay Written by
Richard J. Perry

Poems Written by
Andrea Dietrich

BLACK

>   MALE VOICE (V.O.)
>   The colours in which we love,
>
>   are here...
>
>   there...
>
>   and everywhere.

                                                    CUT TO:

2   EXT. CANARY WARF - DAY   2

JEAN-BAPTISTE (early 30s) He's suited and booted, looking like he's just stepped out of the board room and into the real world.

He's still, stood as the chaos around him moves at the speed of light. Business men and women in suits chaotically interchanging, crashing into each other.

Jean Baptiste starts walking he takes his jacket off, folds it before placing in a nearby bin. Takes his tie off and does the same.

Jean-Baptiste is a man who's only lived by rules, regimented routines and with a structured like attitude to how he lives.

                                                    CUT TO:

2B   EXT. SHOREDITCH HIGH STREET - DAY   2B

SISTINE (early 30s) exits from an art shop. London buses, cyclists and pedestrians all bump and move chaotically in front of her.

Sistine is someone who constantly questions the world and why people do the things they do, the decisions they make. She questions humanities need for material items, always looking for the purest form of emotion.

She turns a corner, exiting.

SUPER:

                   SIX DAYS OF SISTINE

3   EXT. ARNOLD CIRCUS, SHOREDITCH - DAY   3

         We SUPER: **DAY ONE**

         Sistine enters, sits on the bench--

         Watches the people pass her by.

         She reads from an old book.

         Her clothes say only corporate, well presented and very
         structured.

         We stay on Sistine as she watches the world around her.

         Intercutting:

4   IMAGE SEQUENCE: 4

         Sistine is standing in front of a white back drop.

         We cut images of extreme closeups. Eyes, teeth. Hands.

         The details that makes her a person.

         Looks to the lens. Her hand runs through her hair.

         We are seeing the purest form of Sistine. The bare raw
         self before the world and it's problems became who she is
         now.

                            SISTINE (V.O.)
                        (**Cinder Girl**)
                  An ember sparked will softly glow,
                  and fed by fuel, will grow
                  and grow.
                  I once was cinder, sparked by you,
                  first timid. . . till the flames
                  then grew.

                  And so our start was touch of
                  dawn,
                  with amber hue, for I was drawn
                  to eyes so welcoming and warm
                  I never guessed you'd do me harm.

                  Like morning glory, love in June
                  the rapture of mid-afternoon,
                  romance of which the ancients
                  wrote,
                  our passion had no antidote.

                                                     (CONTINUED)

4   CONTINUED: 4

                         And with the dusk, though scarlet
                         tinged,
                         our love began to come unhinged,
                         for clouds arrived, which filled
                         your eyes,
                         extinguishing bright twilight
                         skies.

                         With cold of night came shadows'
                         pall,
                         and I could not tear down your
                         wall.
                         By midnight's hour, the fire was
                         dead.
                         Mere ashes smoldered in its stead.

                         You left, and should you reappear,
                         I've vowed to shun you. Now I
                         fear
                         the very thing for which I yearn -
                         one touch. . . and then again - to
                         burn.

5   EXT. ARNOLD CIRCUS, SHOREDITCH - DAY   5

            Jean-Baptiste climbs the stairs of Arnold Circus,
            reaching the center.

            He gazes over the other side to see Sistine sitting there
            reading on the bench.

            Jean-Baptiste sits on the bench opposite, watches her
            reading. He tries to asses the type of woman she is by
            what she's wearing. He looks at her shoes, her long
            skirt, the way her hair is done up in a bun.

                                                               CUT TO:

6   <u>AGAINST WHITE</u>   6

            We see IMAGES of what Jean Baptiste's perception of her
            is. Sat at a desk, an aggressive person. Yelling into her
            phone. What he doest realize is he's quick to judge...

                                                               CUT TO:

7   EXT. ARNOLD CIRCUS, SHOREDITCH - DAY   7

            Sistine can feel him watching her.

            She looks up.

4.

8   IMAGE SEQUENCE: 8

The same shots as Sistine but now Jean-Baptiste.

Jean Baptiste is standing in front of a white back drop. We cut images of extreme closeups. Eyes, teeth. Hands. The details that makes him a person. Looks to the lens.

We are seeing the purest form of Jean Baptiste. The bare raw self.

                    JEAN-BAPTISTE (V.O.)
          (Find Me in Six - Tranquility)
          Find Me where the summer breeze is
          sighing.

          There time floats me in its
          endless sea.

          Engulfed am I - by sweet
          tranquility.

          On a lofty esplanade, gulls flying

          are trailing clouds through azure,
          wheeling free.

          Sun flashes gold its grin! There
          you'll find me.

9   EXT. ARNOLD CIRCUS, SHOREDITCH - DAY   9

Jean-Baptiste and Sistine stare at each other to the point of losing themselves in each other's eyes.

There's instant chemistry. A gaze into each others souls.

Neither of them knows how to proceed and the moment is intimately calm.

The wind blows across the middle of them and suddenly stops, they both feel and notice the singular gust which ignites Jean Baptiste the desire to take a deep breath as he's worried about stepping forward and making that decision.

There's grace and nervousness from them both, twitching of the fingers.

Sistine runs her hand through her hair in the same way as the image sequence which prompts--

                                                  MATCH CUT TO:

5.

10   IMAGE SEQUENCE: 10

        Against white. Sistine finishes gliding her hand down her
        long hair.

        We follow the hand as it raises forward--

        As though asking the recipient to take it--

                                                          CUT TO:

11   EXT. ARNOLD CIRCUS, SHOREDITCH - DAY   11

        Jean Baptiste continues to make the decision.

        He stares down at her hand.

                            JEAN-BAPTISTE (V.O.)
                        (What Love Is)
                    When Love comes pounding on a
                    drum,
                    it comes on fast and hard and
                    strong
                    until two hearts in synch beat
                    passion's song.

                            SISTINE (V.O.)
                    Sometimes love comes clanging down
                    the tracks.
                    It clashes or it clamors to be
                    heard,
                    so at its crossing, meaning is
                    obscured.

                            JEAN-BAPTISTE (V.O.)
                    Other times, love lurks or it
                    attacks.
                    Unrequited, love can pierce or
                    burn
                    until its ventricle turns into
                    black.

                            SISTINE (V.O.)
                    And then are times love gently
                    climbs
                    or eases sure-footed to one's door
                    or sweetly seeps and saturates the
                    soul.

                            JEAN-BAPTISTE (V.O.)
                    It's strong and yet it's soft.
                    It doesn't sting or snip. It
                    listens
                              (MORE)

                                                        (CONTINUED)

11   CONTINUED: 11
                             JEAN-BAPTISTE (V.O.) (CONT'D)
                     and reverberates the whispers of
                     the heart.

12   IMAGE SEQUENCE: 12

       Against white.

       Jean Baptiste takes her hand--

                                                          CUT TO:

13   EXT. ARNOLD CIRCUS, SHOREDITCH - DAY   13

       Jean-Baptiste finally stands and walks over to her. She
       puts her book down on her lap, allowing Jean-Baptiste to
       sit next to her.

       He smiles--

                             JEAN-BAPTISTE
                         (French accent)
                     Salut, je n'étais pas sûr de
                     savoir comment ou quoi dire. Je
                     m'appelle Jean Baptiste.

                             SISTINE
                         (Spanish accent)
                     Hola, lo siento, no hablo francés.
                     ¿Habla usted Inglés?
                         (then)
                     Mi nombre es Sistine

       Jean-Baptiste shakes his head.

       Both of them realize the predicament. Neither of them can
       speak each other's languages or common English but it
       doesn't matter.

       They share a timid laugh due to the lack of communicative
       ability.

14   IMAGE SEQUENCE: 14

       Against white.

       Jean Baptiste takes her hand and Sistine is pulled into
       frame.

       They stare at each other.

       Holding still as we TRACK toward them.

                                                         (CONTINUED)

14   CONTINUED: 14

                         SISTINE (V.O.)
                    (It Matters Not)
              It hovers here, a moon opaque,
              obscuring mountain trails I take.
              No other living things appear.
              A moon opaque. . . It hovers here.

              I follow on along a ledge;
              below a swirling river's edge.
              In front of me, the canyon's yawn.
              Along a ledge, I follow on.

              I see no hue when fog congeals.
              Oh, doom of one who no more feels!
              The moon has fled, as so have you.
              When fog congeals, I see no hue.

              Now all is dim; it matters not.
              My dear one's heart I have not
              got.
              No use in living without him.
              It matters not. Now all is dim.

              At peace I'll be if I should fall
              to murky water from this wall.
              Oh, yawning canyon, swallow me.
              If I should fall, at peace I'll be

                                                              MATCH CUT TO:

15   EXT. ARNOLD CIRCUS, SHOREDITCH - DAY   15

     The same stare. We've matched to them on the bench.

     A subtle smile and we--

                                                                    CUT TO:

16   EXT. BRICK LANE - DAY   16

     Sistine takes Jean-Baptiste through Brick Lane and East
     London Markets; they stop and look at all the stalls.

     Picking out new clothes, taking closer look at the
     antiques.

     Sistine finds some clothes she admires, they're vibrant
     in colours and much different to what she's currently
     wearing.

     She buys them.

     They grab a bite to eat, some market stall food.

                                                                (CONTINUED)

16   CONTINUED: 16

       Sistine shows him pictures on her phone of the Sistine
       chapel. She points to a young couple opposite them and
       indicates with her hand how they met at the chapel, fell
       in love and that's why she's called Sistine.

       Jean-Baptiste receives a text message, begins to open it
       and read.

       Sistine watches.

       Feeling awkward herself she takes out her phone and reads
       a message, what people seem to do these days to avoid
       comfortable silences.

       Both Jean-Baptiste and Sistine feel annoyed at their
       phones. The message we don't see but it doesn't matter.

       Their expressions say it all, hurt by what's been sent
       through.

       Sistine stands, takes Jean-Baptiste's phone off him and
       smashes them on both the floor. Jean Baptiste holds a
       moment before standing and making sure there's no rubbish
       left on the ground.

       He puts the broken pieces in the bin.

       He's not angry at her but instead left with a sense of
       freedom, all be it very slight.

17   IMAGE SEQUENCE: 17

       Against white we see projected images on Sistine and Jean
       Baptiste-- Holding their arms out in freedom. Tranquil. A
       sense of escape.

18   EXT. BRICK LANE - DAY   18

       They both exit, hand in hand through Brick Lane.

       The CAMERA finds a newspaper cover hanging on the edge of
       the bench in which they sat.

       It blows in the wind but we can just about make the
       writing:

       *"Hedge fund tycoon Fairminer Tomson dies in a tragic
       accident, survived by his only daughter. Soon to inherit
       the million dollar estate."*

                                                          (CONTINUED)

18   CONTINUED: 18

The paper flies out from underneath the bench and up into the sky as we--

DISSOLVE TO:

19   IMAGE SEQUENCE: 19

The white background changes to a light yellow. Jean Baptiste turns and see's two doors.

He steps over to them both. Not being able to decide which one.

```
                    JEAN-BAPTISTE (V.O.)
                (Cinder Girl)
    An ember sparked will softly glow,
    and fed by fuel, will grow
    and grow.
    I once was cinder, sparked by you,
    first timid. . . till the flames
    then grew.

    And so our start was touch of
    dawn,
    with amber hue, for I was drawn
    to eyes so welcoming and warm
    I never guessed you'd do me harm.

    Like morning glory, love in June
    the rapture of mid-afternoon,
    romance of which the ancients
    wrote,
    our passion had no antidote.


    And with the dusk, though scarlet
    tinged,
    our love began to come unhinged,
    for clouds arrived, which filled
    your eyes,
    extinguishing bright twilight
    skies.

    With cold of night came shadows'
    pall,
    and I could not tear down your
    wall.
    By midnight's hour, the fire was
    dead.
    Mere ashes smoldered in its stead.

    You left, and should you reappear,
                (MORE)
```

(CONTINUED)

19   CONTINUED: 19
                                JEAN-BAPTISTE (V.O.) (CONT'D)
                         I've vowed to shun you. Now I
                         fear
                         the very thing for which I yearn -
                         one touch. . . and then again - to
                         burn.

       Jean Baptiste opens the door to the left and steps
       through--

                                                              CUT TO:

20   EXT. LONDON FIELDS - DAY   20

       Sistine and Jean Baptiste end up in London Fields, they
       watch as the people around them are having BBQ's.

       The smoke rays bursting through the trees.

       Jean Baptiste lies there with Sistine lying on top of
       him.

       She twirls a dandelion in front of the sun.

       Watching as the rays shine through the petals.

       The sun begins to fall in the background.

                                SISTINE (V.O.)
                            (Like Cleansing Rain)
                         Such contemplating that the poets
                         do.
                         They sing of God, our spirits to
                         renew.

                         With Mother Nature often they're
                         in tune
                         And offer up their verse to sun
                         and moon.

                         They praise the sunset over a blue
                         lake
                         While pondering man's purpose, and
                         they ache...
                         They ache for all that earth can
                         never be,
                         For dreams they've lost, and for
                         humanity.

                         And when they ache, their words
                         are filled with pain
                         Which pour out from their soul
                         like cleansing rain!

       Sistine turns to Jean-Baptiste.

                                                          (CONTINUED)

20   CONTINUED: 20

        Sits up opposite him.

        She turns to the main road.

        Looks at the exit sign.

        Looks back at Jean-Baptiste.

                                                              CUT TO:

21   EXT. NEWSAGENTS, LONDON FIELDS - DAY   21

        Sistine exits holding an A to Z.

        She looks at the map with Jean-Baptiste and opens it to
        the West Country. BATH, SOMERSET.

        Jean-Baptiste questions the reason as to why there,
        unsure.

        Sistine turns to see a young family outside the market
        stall.

        The father raising his daughter high in the air, smiling
        with her. Happy moments in time.

                                                              CUT TO:

22   EXT. LONDON FIELDS STATION - DAY   22

        Jean-Baptiste and Sistine stand outside the station.

        It's closed till Monday for repairs.

        They step out and find themselves in a predicament, they
        watch as two men get out from a beat up old car.

        Sistine turns to Jean-Baptiste, he shakes his head as
        though to say no.

        The men walk away, the car isn't locked.

        Sistine holds her hand out.

        Trying to establish some form of trust.

        Jean Baptiste still shakes his head.

        He holds a moment, she doesn't move.

        Stillness.

                                                              (CONTINUED)

| 22 | CONTINUED: | 22 |

He looks at her, trying to gauge who she really is and why she feels so comfortable doing this.

She responds with a calm sense of security and confidence.

Jean Baptiste takes a deep breath before taking her hand.

They run over to the car and quickly jump in.

The two men in the background notice as Sistine drives fast away.

They chase them down the street, SCREAMING and running after them but they can't keep up with the car.

CUT TO:

| 23 | EXT/INT. CAR DRIVING - DUSK | 23 |

The car drives out of London and toward the motorway.

Sistine's driving and Jean Baptiste's worried, anxious about what he's just done.

Sistine takes his hand and reassures him.

There's gentle touch, fingers graze each others as her hand stays on the gear shift.

>   JEAN-BAPTISTE (V.O.)
>   **(A Tale of Fire and
>   Ice)**
>   <u>Part I: Ice</u>
>   He shines like silver midnight
>   moon - cool marble statue,
>   this tycoon. And though he makes
>   the ladies swoon, of ice
>   he's hewn.; of ice he's hewn.
>
>   He's poker-faced and can deceive
>   competitors and can achieve
>   most anything, but can't conceive
>   of Genevieve, of Genevieve.
>
>   Like Neptune, distant from the sun
>   - relationships he chose to shun.
>   He thought the search for love was
>   done. He has no one; he has no
>   one.
>
>   Now love's allure has come his
>   way. What will he do? What will he
>   say?
>   (MORE)

(CONTINUED)

23   CONTINUED: 23

                              JEAN-BAPTISTE (V.O.) (CONT'D)
                    Will he grab hold, beg love to
                    stay, or let it stray? Or let it
                    stray?

                    Part II: Fire
                    This dragoness disguised in lace -
                    passion's flower with angel's
                    face,
                    precisely picks the time and place
                    each dream to chase,
                    each dream to chase.

                    Like ink the color red, she stains
                    the hearts of those whose love she
                    drains, and then she leaves when
                    naught remains No lust she feigns;
                    no lust she feigns.

                    And now there's one who would
                    suffice. For him alone, she'd
                    sacrifice her everything, so he of
                    ice she must
                    entice, she must entice.

                    So Genevieve now strikes the
                    flame. Will man of ice his
                    love proclaim? Beneath her fire
                    and his cold frame,
                    they're both the same. They're
                    both the same.

          The car smoothly drives west, heading to Bath.

          The sun skims down from the west. A myriad of reds and
          oranges.

                                                            CUT TO:

24   EXT. CITYSCAPE, BATH, SOMERSET - DAWN   24

          The beautiful architecture of the city of Bath in the
          background.

          SUPER: **DAY TWO**

          The sun beams shining through them as they drift back and
          forth in the wind.

                                                            CUT TO:

14.

25   EXT. CAR, BATH - DAWN   25

        Jean Baptiste and Sistine lie asleep in the car fully
        clothed.

        Sistine awakens and looks at him fondly, he still sleeps.

26   IMAGE SEQUENCE: 26

        Sistine stands in front of the yellow background.

        She's alone. She turns and finds herself in--

        An old quaint countryside estate.

        She walks through the vintage hallways. The aging
        bookshelves. The mahogany furniture.

        Each item has a history.

        She turns to see a pitch black corridor. A single light
        source at the end.

        She questions it with her eyes. Slowly moves toward it.

                            SISTINE (V.O.)
                        **(Star-Crossed - For
                         Love of Day, For the
                         Love of Night)**
                    In shadows' veils, at end of
                    night, sweet Moon removes her
                    modest light and softly, yet
                    again, exhales - at end
                    of night, in shadows' veils.

                    As she departs, her love's
                    released to climb the stairway
                    to the east. They cannot meet to
                    share their hearts.
                    Her love's released as she
                    departs.

                    She watches him while hid from
                    view, the way he kisses
                    morning's dew, and sees gold rays
                    spill from his rim.
                     While hid from view, she watches
                    him.

                    Sad Moon, alone for centuries,
                    with awe has watched
                    Sun leave, cerise. while she,
                    afar. . . how cold she's grown!
                    For centuries, sad moon alone.
                            (MORE)

                                                      (CONTINUED)

26   CONTINUED: 26
                            SISTINE (V.O.) (CONT'D)
                    She takes his place so he may
                    rest. And though forlorn,
                    she's always dressed in lace, for
                    Luna has great grace. So he may
                    rest, she takes his place.

                    For love of night, for love of
                    day, she can't implore him that he
                    sway
                    from course. To be apart's their
                    plight.
                    For love of day, for love of
                    night.

        Sistine turns behind her and watches as the room
        disintegrates into darkness.

        The solid light source becomes brighter and engulfs the
        room with light and dust.

        She smiles as we--

                                                        CUT TO:

27   EXT. CAR, BATH - DAWN   27

        Finally Jean-Baptiste awakens.

        There's a slight feeling of guilt.

        Some awkwardness before finally sitting himself up.

                                                        CUT TO:

28   EXT. BATH SUMMER MARKET - DAY   28

        Much like in Shoreditch previously Sistine and Jean
        Baptiste wade their way through the market stalls.

        Embracing the day, the items around them.

        They dance their way through.

        Glimpses of romanticism forms between them--

        The soft touches of each other's skin--

        The idiosyncrasies of nervous grace--

        Withdrawal of moments but then succumbing to their
        desires--

                                                        (CONTINUED)

28   CONTINUED: 28

       Delicate bumps of body parts--

       Interlocking of fingers--

       Each time they get closer and closer they have to
       withdraw.

29   IMAGE SEQUENCE: 29

       An empty ballroom. A single light source.

       Jean Baptiste and Sistine dance around the room, a slow
       waltz.

       A dance of grace.

                         JEAN-BAPTISTE (V.O.)
                     (Life is a Dance)
                 Life is a dance we were all born
                 to do. The styles to choose
                 from are more than a few! Some
                 choose simple two-step;
                 some move with flair. Some slow
                 dance; some break dance,
                 devil-may-care! Some free style,
                 while others just dance on cue.

                 Some tango with zest; some shuffle
                 soft-shoe. Others glide easily,
                 waltzing on through. Some change
                 their partners; some stay
                 one pair. Life is a dance.

                 You start with the styles in your
                 own milieu, then grow as
                 you add on new moves you view.
                 You'll stumble, but
                 sometimes dance on sweet air! Just
                 keep the beat; try new
                 steps if you dare, for where you
                 end up
                 is all up to you. . . Life is a
                 dance!

       They stop.

       Jean Baptiste turns to look behind him--

       A Dark Corner-- we hear the sound of CHILDREN'S LAUGHTER.
       We hear a montage of Kitchen CLATTERING.

       BLENDERS BUZZING

       WASHING MACHINES TURNER

                                                          (CONTINUED)

29   CONTINUED: 29

            WEDDING BELLS RINGING

            A SCREAMING MATCH BETWEEN MAN AND WOMAN.

            The Scream becomes LOUDER and LOUDER, Jean Baptiste looks
            petrified before we--

                                                                    CUT TO:

30   EXT. CAR, BATH - EVENING   30

            As the day draws to a close. Sistine sits on the car
            bonnet.

            Jean Baptiste in the far distance.

31   EXT. BATH - SAME TIME   31

            Jean-Baptiste exchanges his watch for some food from the
            market seller.

            He looks at it one last time.

            Turns it over and reads the inscription.

            We can't see whom its from but know it's of sentimental
            importance to him.

            He takes a breath and hands it over to the seller.

            The seller gives him an entire shopping basket filled
            with food.

            There's an exchange of thanks.

            Jean Baptiste makes his way back to Sistine and as he
            reaches her he throws her a sandwich, which she opens
            without hesitation, as she hasn't eaten all day.

            Jean Baptiste walks round to the back of the car to open
            up the boot, about to put the rest of the food in.

            His face falls.

            He can't move.

            He looks over to Sistine and she returns with a look of
            uncertainty.

            It's from what he's looking at does he truly think that
            this has he gone too far.

32   IMAGE SEQUENCE: 32

        Jean Baptiste stands front of a new build standard
        suburban house.

        The "For Sale" sign still outside.

        He stares long and hard at the door. Its the same door
        that he chose not to enter into in the white sequence.

                            JEAN-BAPTISTE (V.O.)
                         (A Home Sweet Home)
                    At long day's end, our thoughts
                    may stray to where
                    we long to wend our way- a
                    peaceful place where we
                    dismiss all things in life that
                    are amiss, and none are
                    wont to cause dismay.

                    Our footsteps hasten us to this:
                    the warmth of hearth,
                    the welcome kiss. For those less
                    fortunate I pray a home
                    sweet home they'll find one day.

                                                            CUT TO:

33   EXT. BATH - SAME TIME   33

        Jean Baptiste continues to look at Sistine then back at
        the boot.

        Sistine's curiosity leads her round to the back of the
        car.

        She looks at what Jean Baptiste is looking at.

        A guitar lies flat in the boot.

        Sistine doesn't understand what the big deal is, she
        looks up at him.

        Jean Baptiste covers his hand and turns the guitar over.

        Revealing millions of pounds worth of small white
        packets.

        Sistine pushes him out of the way and closes the boot
        door.

        Jean Baptiste is again anxious and worried.

        He begins trembling and shaking.

                                                          (CONTINUED)

33   CONTINUED: 33

       Sistine grabs his hand to stop it.

       Looks at him with certainty that it's going to be okay.

       She comforts his fear.

       She strokes his cheek with gentle touch which calms him
       down.

34   IMAGE SEQUENCE: 34

       Jean Baptiste is surround by strobes. The light is
       pounding down on him.

       The strobing splashing across his face.

       Within each splash of light we're presented with a
       CHILD'S LAUGHTER.

       A SCREAMING BABY.

       A mortgage bill flies past him. Almost hitting him.

       He's surrounded in unpredictable chaos which he hates.

                          SISTINE (V.O.)
                       (The Nail Biter)
                 He bites his nails beside me on
                 the bed so loudly!
                 This strange habit is most
                 grating. I'd like to throw a
                 pillow
                 at his head, but he would just
                 continue, not abating.

                 I'm used to just how vexing he can
                 get, like when he begs
                 for food that I am eating. When
                 someone comes to call,
                 he gets upset; then settles down
                 and gives a gleeful greeting -

                 Unless the visitor is someone
                 small! He sits and stares if I
                 pick up a child then panics if the
                 infant starts to bawl. I love my
                 sweetie though he gets so wild!
                 Although a naughty child
                 himself is he, how sweet and
                 trusting is his love for me.

                                                         CUT TO:

35   INT. CAR - EVENING   35

            Jean Baptiste is wide-awake with Sistine asleep by his
            side. He looks up at the stars, what has he gotten
            himself into. Is there a point of return? What should he
            do?

            He's constantly debating with himself.

            He looks at her, then back up to the stars in
            disappointment with himself.

            Who is she? How is she so calm? Is she leading him down a
            wrong path?

            Slowly Jean-Baptiste removes Sistine's arm from around
            his chest and gets out the car slowly.

36   EXT. CAR - CONTINUOUS   36

            Jean Baptiste opens the boot again.

            He covers his hand with his sleeve and slowly goes
            through the small packets.

            He finds in the guitar case a business card. An address
            on it but nothing else. He places the card in his sock
            and closes the boot up again.

            Gazes through the window at Sistine.

            His lust and desire overwhelming his decisions.

37   IMAGE SEQUENCE: 37

            The end of the strobing... they begin to slow down and
            the light brightly shines in one spot.

            Sistine stands in front of Jean Baptiste.

            There's a moments calm before--

            We FLASH CUT to an image of him kissing her with ultimate
            passion and raw animalistic intensity.

            The room changes into a deep Red.

            Suddenly the dark and deep passionate red turns back to
            white and we--

                                                          CUT TO:

21.

38   EXT. CAR - CONTINUOUS   38

        Jean Baptiste stares back at Sistine.

        We've seen what he wants to do but doesn't.

        He returns to his calm state.

        Opens the door and enters back into the car.

                                                            CUT TO:

39   EXT. HUGE ESTATE, BATH, SOMERSET- DAWN   39

        We see a stunning estate, the large gates restrict any
        one from getting in.

        SUPER: **DAY THREE**

40   EXT. HUGE ESTATE, BATH, SOMERSET - DAWN   40

        We TRACK back to reveal Sistine sat on the bonnet of her
        car.

        Jean Baptiste stood next to her.

        She can't ring the doorbell.

        She doesn't want to.

        The plaque on the side of the gates reads "Thomson
        Residence"

        There's just a moments waiting.

        Debating going through her mind as she stares at the
        gates.

41   IMAGE SEQUENCE: 41

        Sistine is running through a crop field.

        The sense of freedom. Her arms stretched out, reaching
        for the empty space out in front of her. The images we
        saw projected on her earlier but now full screen.

        There is nothing but pure nature all around her.

        Empty.

        Freedom

                                                        (CONTINUED)

41   CONTINUED: 22.
                                                                         41

                             SISTINE (V.O.)
                         (Winter Blues)
                    Another year has come - chillingly
                    - and more
                    chillingly for me than in decades
                    heretofore.
                    I watch it ranting from my window
                    as I recall. . . .

                    The year already past had tugged
                    me from those
                    tame and toasty days when I lay
                    face up to sun dreaming
                    that my summer would never end. It
                    brought me to this
                    winter when it withered up and
                    died, but half a century
                    and more of memories had fallen
                    for me by now. Like
                    pretty crystal flakes they fell,
                    drifting through my mind -
                    places, events and people.

                    Oh, those people I looked up to in
                    my youth - fallen as the
                    snow! How many pretty snow flakes
                    have melted now away?
                    Only my memories of them remain. .
                    . memories
                    now piled up like snowdrifts in my
                    brain.
                    Yes, the newborn year has arrived.
                    Just one month old and
                    already, it has lost its crawl.
                    This infant's aging process
                    parallels, on the larger scale,
                    that fleeting span of time known
                    as life - a time that all the
                    living undergo.

                    The new year carries on (as must
                    we all) to soon
                    complete its cycle. Let it
                    bluster. Let it wail. Let it
                    rattle
                    at my door, for soon enough, all
                    signs of it will cease.

     Suddenly within the empty field the clouds above begin to
     merge together.

     There's THUNDER--

     DARKNESS--

                                                              (CONTINUED)

41   CONTINUED: (2)   41

       And the RAIN pounds down as we--

                                                           CUT TO:

42   EXT. HUGE ESTATE, BATH, SOMERSET - DAWN   42

       Sistine finally stands and steps round the car to get in
       the driving seat.

       Jean Baptiste follows into the passenger seat.

       He comforts her.

       She turns the ENGINE on and drives away.

                                                           CUT TO:

43   EXT. CAR - AFTERNOON   43

       The car glides through the streets of Bath.

44   EXT. CITYSCAPE, BATH, SOMERSET- AFTERNOON   44

       The day is almost drawing a close, Sistine pulls up in
       the car, exits and walks into the fields.

       This is the same field as when they first entered in
       Bath.

       The scenic view in the background.

       The trees blowing in the wind.

       Sistine falls to the ground in upset.

       Jean Baptiste slowly makes his way over to her.

       Wraps his arms around her, holding tight.

       He doesn't need to do anything else but just be there for
       her. Just let her be angry and upset.

       He doesn't try to do anything to fix it--

       Instead not trying to fix the problem he simply and
       selflessly holds her in comfort, lets her vulnerability
       leave her body.

       It's the kindest thing he knows what to do.

       They sit there in the fields.

                                                        (CONTINUED)

44   CONTINUED:

                    SISTINE (V.O.)
                (**Cinder Girl**)
          An ember sparked will softly glow,
          and fed by fuel, will grow and
          grow.
          I once was cinder, sparked by you,
          first timid. . . till the flames
          then grew.

                    JEAN-BAPTISTE (V.O.)
          And so our start was touch of
          dawn,
          with amber hue, for I was drawn
          to eyes so welcoming and warm
          I never guessed you'd do me harm.

                    SISTINE (V.O.)
          Like morning glory, love in June
          the rapture of mid-afternoon,
          romance of which the ancients
          wrote,
          our passion had no antidote.

                    JEAN-BAPTISTE (V.O.)
          And with the dusk, though scarlet
          tinged,
          our love began to come unhinged,
          for clouds arrived, which filled
          your eyes,
          extinguishing bright twilight
          skies.

                    SISTINE (V.O.)
          With cold of night came shadows'
          pall,
          and I could not tear down your
          wall.
          By midnight's hour, the fire was
          dead.
          Mere ashes smoldered in its stead.

                    JEAN-BAPTISTE (V.O.)
          You left, and should you reappear,
          I've vowed to shun you. Now I
          fear
          the very thing for which I yearn -
          one touch. . . and then again - to
          burn.

Day becomes evening--

Evening becomes night--

Still they are held in the same position.

25.

45   EXT. CITYSCAPE, BATH, SOMERSET - DUSK   45

         Finally Sistine breaks free from Jean Baptiste.

         There's a long pause of uncertainty.

         Jean Baptiste isn't sure as to what she's thinking of doing.

         She removes her top.

         Implying she wants further comfort.

         Jean Baptiste isn't sure.

         Sistine begins to rub his cheek softly with her hand, nothing but pure grace.

         He takes her hand off his and kisses it.

         He takes his shirt of as they sit there opposite each other, their raw selves.

         Their clear selves.

         No persona, no mask.

         Just them.

         Near naked in body and mind.

         We see premonitions of them and what they want--

46   IMAGE SEQUENCE: 46

         White empty space, darkens again to Red.

         A deep contrast of Reds, blacks and whites surround the space.

         Kisses and delicate touches but then cutting back to reality.

                                                         CUT TO:

47   EXT. CITYSCAPE, BATH, SOMERSET - DUSK   47

         Jean Baptiste and Sistine remain in their previous position.

                                                     (CONTINUED)

		26.
47	CONTINUED:	47

Instead of going through with their lustful desires with each other they decide to just hold each other and fall asleep underneath the stars.

CUT TO:

48	EXT. CITYSCAPE, BATH, SOMERSET - NIGHT	48

Jean Baptiste is lying awake.

Not trembling, not anxious but now in a more familiar sense of calm and peace.

Sistine lies asleep next to him.

Jean Baptiste stands, lifting Sistine up from the ground, she beings to awaken but he SHUSHES her.

He guides her into the car

SUPER: **DAY FOUR**

CUT TO:

49	INT. CAR - NIGHT	49

It's barely gone midnight and the car is streaming though the motorway.

Jean Baptiste driving--

Sistine asleep beside him--

He gazes at her.

He's doing this for her, stepping up and being confident for her.

The soft break lights in front of him from the traffic begin to move and the Red Car lights widen, engulfing the SCREEN as we--

CUT TO:

50	IMAGE SEQUENCE:	50

Jean Baptiste stands in the middle of a busy street.

Cars fly past him at the speed of light.

It's the same car he's driving which is all the cars flying past him. All the same car.

(CONTINUED)

| 50 | CONTINUED: | 50 |

The chaos of the traffic is the chaos in which he is about to embark on.

> JEAN-BAPTISTE (V.O.)
> (Song for My Love, My Sweet)
> At last you've come for me, my love, my sweet! You've come through tranquil woodland, with the breeze, along that path where once we used to meet and with the sunlight streaming through the trees!
>
> With passion in your eyes and wings for feet, you've come for me, and all my anguish flees. You are so near, I hear your wild heart beat. You've come for me, my own wild heart to seize.
>
> Alas! The woods have vanished with the gleam of my waking dawn. It was but a dream.

CUT TO:

| 51 | EXT. LONDON - NIGHT | 51 |

The car streams its way though the bright lights, the intensity of the city.

No longer will Jean Baptiste run from his problems--

He will confront them head on and deal with them.

He will show Sistine that by doing this she can do this with her own family issues--

CUT TO:

| 52 | EXT. HACKNEY WICK - NIGHT | 52 |

The streets are filled with partygoers and those out for their nights of temporary memories.

Jean Baptiste pulls up outside a warehouse.

He pulls out the card he kept in his sock and makes sure he has the right address.

Looks at Sistine who still sleeps on the passenger side.

(CONTINUED)

52   CONTINUED: 52

        He kisses her head with affection before taking a deep
        breath; getting himself ready he opens the car door.

53   EXT. CAR - NIGHT   53

        Jean Baptiste opens the book and brings out the guitar--

        Filled with the packets.

54   EXT. WAREHOUSE - NIGHT   54

        Jean Baptiste heads to the warehouse--

        KNOCKS on the shutter.

        The slat opens and he's seen to have the guitar case in
        his hand.

55   INT. WAREHOUSE - NIGHT   55

        Jean Baptiste steps inside and is greeted by two large
        men.

        They point him the direction of down the hall.

        The heavy DRUM AND BASS music blasts from the PA.

        He continues walking...

                          JEAN-BAPTISTE (V.O.)
                      (At the End of the
                          Rainbow)
                    At the end of the rainbow, dreams
                    unfold. And some people
                    say there is a pot of gold.

                    How well I recall a rainbow one
                    day that shone in the
                    sky when a storm went away.

                    Rain pelted my car; I felt so
                    afraid. But as I neared home, it
                    started
                    to fade. The sky, once so dark,
                    grew more and more blue. I
                    thrilled next to see a rainbow
                    arch through!

                    It bent toward the mountains, so
                    beautiful, a peace and great
                    joy welled up in my soul. No pot
                    of gold at its end did I see, but
                              (MORE)

                                                        (CONTINUED)

55 CONTINUED:

>   JEAN-BAPTISTE (V.O.) (CONT'D)
>   still there was gold and it
>   beckoned to me.
>
>   The mountains were gilded with a
>   bright gleam. This is
>   the magic that makes poets dream!
>
>   When I got home, I took paper and
>   pen
>   and wrote of that beauty, God's
>   promise to men.
>
>   Again I recall how my soul lifted.
>   At the rainbow's end, God's love
>   is gifted.

As Jean Baptiste reaches the end of the hall he's forced to sit down opposite a man in the shadows.

There's no movement.

Nothing.

The man in the shadows throws a photograph down on the table in front of Jean-Baptiste.

The photo is of Sistine and him in Bath--

Jean Baptiste realizes they have been monitoring them the whole time.

Jean Baptiste places the guitar down on the table.

Moves his hand to indicate this matter is resolved.

The man in the shadows does nothing.

Finally there's some movement and the man in the shadows presents another photo.

This time of Sistine--

Holds it up high--

He sets it alight--

Throws it at Jean Baptiste.

The two men from whom originally drove the car step into the room.

There's no escape for Jean Baptiste.

(CONTINUED)

55   CONTINUED: (2)   55

            They grab him by the collar and hold him up against the
            wall. The aggression on their faces say it all as to
            whats coming for Jean Baptiste.

56   EXT. WAREHOUSE - NIGHT   56

            Jean Baptiste is thrown out from the warehouse, bruised
            and beaten to near death.

            He falls into a large puddle, surrounded by dirt.

            Sistine races out from the car to comfort him, aid him.

            Lies down on his back and looks up at the stars as we--

                                                          CUT TO:

57   EXT. CITYSCAPE, BATH, SOMERSET - NIGHT   57

            Jean Baptiste is lying awake again. Matching the cut to
            earlier.

            Not trembling, not anxious but now in a more familiar
            sense of calm and peace.

            He gazes up at the stars.

            We learn that the whole going back to London scenario was
            a thought process going through his mind. A way to tell
            himself that problems can't be run from. But have to be
            tackled head on.

            A symbolic act of making his world more interesting.

            Sistine lies asleep next to him. Her eye lids flicker
            like the London scenario was a dream to her. We intercut
            the images as her eyes flicker in dream sleep.

            Jean Baptiste closes his eyes and we--

                                                      MATCH CUT TO:

58   EXT. CITYSCAPE, BATH, SOMERSET - DAWN   58

            Where Jean Baptiste awakens.

            Sistine walks from the distance.

            Some food from the car and gifts it to Jean Baptiste.

            She moves into him and allows him to wrap his arms around
            her.

59	IMAGE SEQUENCE:	59

The white room is empty.

Jean Baptiste sits in the middle.

Calm.

But at a distance.

He holds his pose.

He stands, proud and confident.

Steps forward and another version of himself remains behind him.

Small and physically withdrawn.

He's mentally become a new man.

                    JEAN-BAPTISTE (V.O.)
             (It Matters Not)
It hovers here, a moon opaque,
obscuring mountain trails I take.
No other living things appear.
A moon opaque. . . It hovers here.

I follow on along a ledge;
below a swirling river's edge.
In front of me, the canyon's yawn.
Along a ledge, I follow on.

I see no hue when fog congeals.
Oh, doom of one who no more feels!
The moon has fled, as so have you.
When fog congeals, I see no hue.

Now all is dim; it matters not.
My dear one's heart I have not got.
No use in living without him.
It matters not. Now all is dim.

At peace I'll be if I should fall
to murky water from this wall.
Oh, yawning canyon, swallow me.
If I should fall, at peace I'll be.

                                        CUT TO:

32.

60   EXT. CITYSCAPE, BATH, SOMERSET - DAWN   60

             Sistine looks up at Jean Baptiste.

             She knows what she needs to do.

61   IMAGE SEQUENCE: 61

             The white room is empty.

             Sistine sits in the middle.

             Calm.

             But at a distance.

             She holds her pose.

             She stands, proud and confident.

             Steps forward and another version of herself remains
             behind her.

             She mentally become a new woman.

                                 SISTINE (V.O.)
                               (A Home Sweet Home)
                        At long day's end, our thoughts
                        may stray to
                        where we long to wend our way- a
                        peaceful place
                        where we dismiss all things in
                        life that are amiss,
                        and none are wont to cause dismay.

                        Our footsteps hasten us to this:
                        the warmth of hearth,
                        the welcome kiss. For those less
                        fortunate I pray a home
                        sweet home they'll find one day.

                                                                 CUT TO:

62   EXT. CITYSCAPE, BATH, SOMERSET - DAWN   62

             Jean Baptiste recognizes this within her.

             He graces her cheek much in the same way she's done to
             him.

             He heads back over to the car and lifts the boot door.

             He smiles as the items inside are no longer there.

                                                              (CONTINUED)

62   CONTINUED: 62

       He realizes that he doesn't need sub plots added to his
       life to make it more interesting--

       He just needs to embrace it.

       Sistine and the emotive responses and the way they can
       find peace and comfort in each others embrace is all that
       is needed in life.

       He shuts the boot.

                                                         CUT TO:

63   EXT. BATH, SOMERSET - DAY   63

       Sistine and Jean Baptiste walk through the inner city.

       The rustic architecture around them.

       Holding each other in embrace.

       He can feel her distancing herself from him.

                           JEAN-BAPTISTE (V.O.)
                       (A Tribute to a Star)
                   On you the angels did bestow a
                   glow your friends
                   would come to know as star-shine!

                   For even stars cannot outshine
                   your countenance.
                   It's as divine as starlight.

                   Oh, how you hush those stars, my
                   dear, from brightly
                   shining when you're near; they're
                   star-struck.

                   I too am stricken by your sight.
                   I'd love to be with you all night
                   to star-gaze.

                   Shine on, sweet man, but do not
                   burn too long or strongly;
                   stars might turn to stardust!

       Jean Baptiste reaches a market stall that sells red
       roses; he purchases one just to lift a smile from
       Sistine.

       She does and reacts fondly of the gesture, but it's
       tainted with an impending distant reaction.

                                                      (CONTINUED)

63   CONTINUED: 34.
                                                                63

She tries to hide it from Jean Baptiste but he can feel it from her.

                                                           CUT TO:

64   INT. CAR, BATH - NIGHT   64

Both Jean Baptiste and Sistine are wide awake.

There's a distance between them.

Not the fond embrace they usually have.

Her mind is overwhelmed with uncertainty and it's something that Jean Baptiste doesn't want to delve into and find out.

                                                           CUT TO:

65   EXT. CITYSCAPE, BATH, SOMERSET - DAWN   65

Jean Baptiste awakens.

The car is empty.

Sistine has gone.

He steps out of the car; Sistine is nowhere to be found.

SUPER: **DAY FIVE**

Jean Baptiste takes a deep breath and understands where she's gone.

66   IMAGE SEQUENCE: 66

The two doors in the distance.

Jean Baptiste steps out from the left door and heads into the right.

                    JEAN-BAPTISTE (V.O.)
                (In Solitude)
          In solitude, I watch the clear
          blue sky. Leaves flutter on the
          grand majestic oak beneath which I
          am sitting;
          swallows fly around me, swooping!

          Now I hear a croak - a sound that
          I am sure I'd never
                         (MORE)

                                                      (CONTINUED)

66   CONTINUED: 66
                              JEAN-BAPTISTE (V.O.) (CONT'D)
                         hear if I were on a busy city
                         street. I stand and walk around.
                         The sound is near. The feeling
                         that I get is rather sweet when
                         finally I spot there on the pond
                         the tiny frog that's serenading
                         me.

                         Crops rippling in the breeze I see
                         beyond my shaded spot. I soon
                         must leave my tree. Red sunset I
                         will watch before I creep in
                         quiet of the night back home to
                         sleep!

                                                              CUT TO:

67   EXT. HUGE ESTATE - DAY   67

       Jean Baptiste stands outside the house.

       He can see through the gaps in the gate Sistine.

       She's holding a young child, a suited man's arm wrapped
       around her.

       Jean Baptiste exits without her noticing.

       She lifts her head to look outside, but her attention is
       brought back to the child in front of her.

       It's clear we see she is back with her family.

                                                              CUT TO:

68   EXT. MOTORWAY - DAY   68

       Jean Baptiste drives back toward London.

69   INT. CAR - DAY   69

       A smile on his face.

       Ordinarily it would be of loss but she opened his eyes to
       freedom rather than the restrictions he's previously
       placed in his life.

       We see images of their time together.

       Their closeness, their bond.

       Their affection.

                                                         (CONTINUED)

69   CONTINUED: 69

Even if it wasn't love in the romantic sense.

It was love in the sense they were drawn together through a need for each other in that particular time in their lives.

70   EXT. LONDON FIELDS - DAY   70

Jean Baptiste returns the car back where they found it.

Walks away.

       SISTINE (V.O.)
    (Kiss The Rain)
I stand here by the lakeshore, and I smell fresh
honeysuckle as I kiss the rain. A memory that I cannot
curtail wafts bitter sweetly to me, and again it's May. . .
the night you came to me by moonlight.
The air was permeated by perfume from blossoms colored innocently white.

But now it's summer; yellow is each
bloom. When plump upon the vines, sweet berries,
red, will be swooped up by birds and
carried away. I stoop to touch a stem.
How soon has fled my flowered youth, and now this day chilled grey, I bow in
downpour like the vines bent low while raindrops turn
to tears and - glistening - flow.

            CUT TO:

71   INT. CORPORATE OFFICE - DAY   71

Jean Baptiste is sat there in a board meeting; he's dressed smart again.

We see his business card: "JOHN BAPDEN"

All proper and structured.

            (CONTINUED)

                                                                37.
    71   CONTINUED: 71

            Opposite him are the two large men and the man who
            threatened him in the Hackney Warehouse. Before his
            imagination of using his work colleagues as his enemies
            in his fantasy.

            SUPER: **DAY SIX**

                                                           CUT TO:

    72   EXT. OFFICE - DAY   72

            Whilst a few office workers are all smoking on a break
            Jean Baptiste edges away from them.

            Looking out onto the London skyline.

            Taking in the air.

            A text message beeps on his phone, a voicemail. He
            listens:

                                FEMALE VOICE (O.S.)
                        *Hey hun, I'm back. I hope you had
                        a good few days without me. I
                        tried calling a few times but
                        can't get through. I hope it's
                        okay I called your work phone.*
                                (then)
                        *Look I've been thinking that the
                        courtyard is going to be fully
                        booked for months on end and so I
                        think we should take the Ivy while
                        we can, Dad said he'd front the
                        deposit so at least we know that
                        the reception will be shared with
                        all our friends. Also you need to
                        get fitted for your tux so let me
                        know and I'll arrange for you. Oh
                        and the cake, decide on a cake
                        will you please. I've sent you
                        many photos so please decide. Love
                        you!*

            Jean Baptiste puts his phone back in his pocket.

            Thinks to himself.

                                                           CUT TO:

    73   INT. OFFICE - DAY   73

            Jean Baptiste steps in and hands a piece of paper onto
            the desk of a weathered man.

                                                        (CONTINUED)

73   CONTINUED: 73

We can read the first line. *"My letter of resignation"*

                    JEAN-BAPTISTE (V.O.)
                (**Cinder Girl**)
    An ember sparked will softly glow,
    and fed by fuel, will grow and
    grow.
    I once was cinder, sparked by you,
    first timid. . . till the flames
    then grew.

    And so our start was touch of
    dawn,
    with amber hue, for I was drawn
    to eyes so welcoming and warm
    I never guessed you'd do me harm.

    Like morning glory, love in June
    the rapture of mid-afternoon,
    romance of which the ancients
    wrote,
    our passion had no antidote.

    And with the dusk, though scarlet
    tinged,
    our love began to come unhinged,
    for clouds arrived, which filled
    your eyes,
    extinguishing bright twilight
    skies.

    With cold of night came shadows'
    pall,
    and I could not tear down your
    wall.
    By midnight's hour, the fire was
    dead.
    Mere ashes smoldered in its stead.

    You left, and should you reappear,
    I've vowed to shun you. Now I
    fear
    the very thing for which I yearn -
    one touch. . . and then again - to
    burn.

                                                    CUT TO:

74   EXT. ARNOLD CIRCUS, LONDON - DAY   74

Where Jean Baptiste and Sistine first met.

Jean Baptiste climbs the stairs to see Sistine there,
wearing similar clothes as she did when they first met.

                                               (CONTINUED)

74   CONTINUED: 74

She smiles at him, he reciprocates with understanding why she left him alone.

He slowly moves towards her, their heads touch--

Look at each others lips--

Wanting the one thing they never got to do--

The passion and desire begins to plague their minds--

      JEAN-BAPTISTE
   (English)
 I love you.

      SISTINE
   (English)
 No you don't. I'm just what you needed. And you're just what I needed.
   (then)
 We made each other realize what's important.
   (then)
 Sometimes moments of reinvention is a good thing... it reminds you who you really are

We see reprises of them speaking in foreign accents.

But both now with English accents and both revealing whom they really are with dialogue.

There's no shock behind the revelation.

Just unity.

      JEAN-BAPTISTE
 Love is a colour wheel Sistine.
   (then)
 The way we feel about our family, the way we feel about our partners, the way we feel lust, monotony, passion, desire, comfortability, friendship, trust, unity...
   (then)
 Love to me is not one thing...
   (then)
 Different love is like colours.
   (then)
 You and I just found the matching one at the right time.

      (CONTINUED)

74   CONTINUED: (2)   74

       She takes his hand, holds it tight.

       With care and understanding--

                           SISTINE
                 In that case...
                     (then)
                 I love you.

       They stare into each others eyes.

       Their souls.

       Two people becoming one.

       The looks at each others lips, the sun slowly falling in
       the background.

       They move into each other to kiss as we--

                                                          CUT TO:

75   BLACK   75

       <u>END CREDITS</u>

- MUSIC LIST -

BY
TONY ANDERSON

BUTTERFLIES - (PIANO SONATA)

FINDING YOUR HEART

YOUR SCARS ARE LIGHTS

YOUNGER

WEAKNESS IS THE WAY

SPIRIT (REMASTERED)

FINDING YOUR HEART (SOLO PIANO)

DIANA

ALL IS NOT LOST

BUTTERFLIES - (NIGHTHAWK REMIX)

HOME

SPIRITEAUX

RISE (AMBIENT PIANO MIX)

DREAMS AND VISIONS

BUTTERFLIES

- ABSTRACT INFLUENCES -

SHOOTING IN SLOW MOTION, CAPTURING THE COMING TOGETHER
OF JEAN BAPTISTE AND SISTINE, IMAGINING THEIR LUST FOR ONE ANOTHER.

BOTH SISTINE AND JEAN BAPTISTE ONLY IMAGINE THEIR PASSION FOR EACH OTHER.
THEIR REALITIES HOWEVER ARE QUITE DIFFERENT.

WHEN WE SEE SOMEONE WE FEEL PASSION FOR WE ONLY IMAGINE LOSING OURSELVES IN THEM.
WHEN WE TRY TO ESCAPE THE PRESSURES OF REALITY.

(WE DO NOT OWN THESE IMAGES, HOWEVER THEY WERE USED FOR INSPIRATION ONLY AND ARE NOT IN THE FINISHED FILM)

- ABSTRACT INFLUENCES -

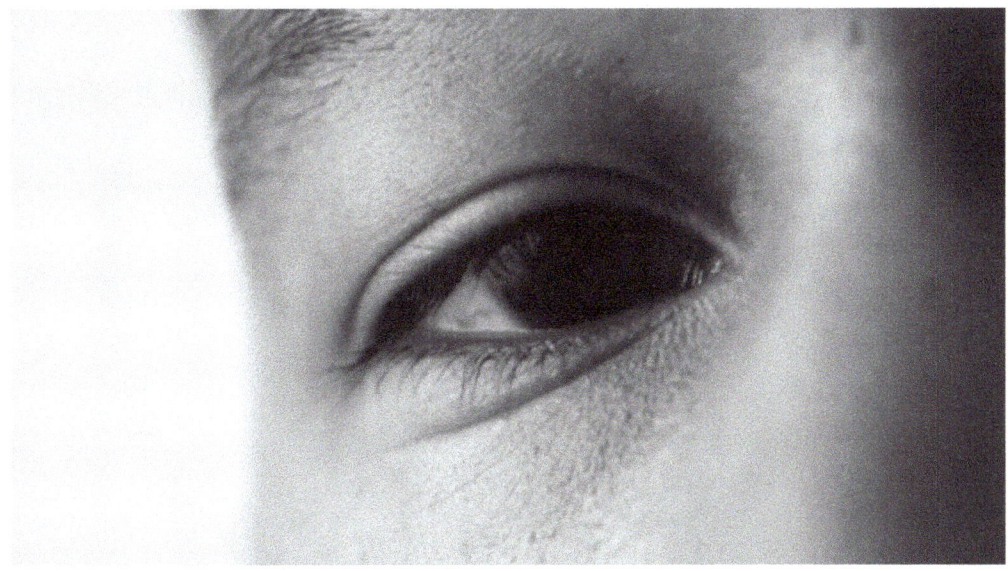

(WE DO NOT OWN THESE IMAGES, HOWEVER THEY WERE USED FOR INSPIRATION ONLY AND ARE NOT IN THE FINISHED FILM)

- SPECIAL THANKS -

BARBARA PERRY | JOHN BUCKLEY | DARREN SMITH | PETE MOORE
HAYLEY WALLACE | FAYE MITCHELL | MERVYN GERRARD | JULIA MORGAN
JESSICA SCOTT | ALISON LIVINGSTONE | ANNAMARIA PENNAZZI
LISA JACOBS | ANNA PAMPHILON

SIMON BERESFORD | DANIEL ALBERT | PIERS NIMMO | ALI SPENCER | JOHN GRANT
NICOLA VAN GELDER | DEBORAH CHARLTON | ANDY HERRITY | NICKY JAMES
ALEXANDRA HARPER | EMMA-ROSE BURGESS | MILA MALTSEV
DAVID PINNEGAR | ANNE-NOELLE PINNEGAR
LYNSEY WINDERS | PHIL WINDERS | LAURA SENIOR | CLARE HILL

THE ROYAL OAK COLUMBIA ROAD | HARE AND HOUNDS
THE OLD KINGS HEAD | THE WEST GATE | PAUL GUY | THE REAL SISTINE
VIRGINIE FABRE | OMAR SEQUERA

BFI | FILM LONDON | BATH FILM OFFICE
CANAL AND RIVER TRUST | PINEWOOD STUDIOS

Six Days of Sistine

www.ingramcontent.com/pod-product-compliance
Lightning Source LLC
Chambersburg PA
CBHW061057170426
43194CB00025B/2962